Maximum Return, Minimum Risk: A Practical Approach

Third Edition

By James B. Cloonan, Ph.D.

American Association of Individual Investors
625 North Michigan Avenue
Chicago, Illinois 60611
(312) 280-0170; (800) 428-2244
www.aaii.com
ISBN: 978-1-883328-26-9   Rev-3

Preface

Over the years, a volume of literature has been written on investment risk, a large part of it extremely technical. While the concept of risk is fairly straightforward and most of us know what it means in many circumstances, it becomes much more complex when we try to quantify it.

Risk comes into play with the simplest of games—a coin toss, roulette, craps—where the odds are reasonably easy to determine and static. It becomes more complex with games like blackjack where the odds change as cards are played. In games like poker and bridge, the pure odds are changed with knowledge of the previous behavior of opponents. However, all of these are simple compared to the multi-faceted probabilities of real-world investing.

Investment risk and its measurement are complex because the risk we take will occur in a future we cannot know. Using past experience, however, we can make estimates by both analytic means and common sense that will give us some understanding of and control over the risk of our portfolios. Attaining that degree of understanding and control is the purpose of this book.

While many of the concepts I discuss here have a mathematical foundation, I have tried to keep the math out of the main body of the analysis for clarity. The statistical underpinnings are important, however, and are presented in Appendix A. The notations A1, A2, etc., indicate mathematical explanations that are found in

Appendix A. In addition to the equations in Appendix A, we also present, where possible, an easy way to perform computerized analysis using an Excel spreadsheet program.

Individual stock selection is not discussed in this book. While risk control involves making some choices in the methods used in selecting asset classes and individual stocks, the approaches to risk control in this book assume you have chosen a strategy for selecting individual assets, whether by your own analysis or using another's methods.

I thank the AAII analytic and editorial staffs for all of their help in the preparation of this book. The content, analysis, and any errors herein are my own and reflect my own biases and opinions. There are many who would disagree with me, and there are other approaches for the control of risk not covered here that other analysts would consider important.

I have made considerable effort to keep this book short and understandable. It is my hope that it will prove helpful on a day-to-day basis as you try to balance the desire to obtain maximum return on your portfolio with the need to control the riskiness of your assets.

This third edition updates examples and expands on concepts introduced in the first two editions.

James B. Cloonan, Ph.D.
February 15, 2011
Chicago, Illinois

Table of Contents

Introduction

"If I pick good stocks, why should I be concerned with risk?" This is a question asked by many individual investors either out loud or to themselves. Most investors don't want to think about risk—sometimes for psychological reasons, sometimes because they don't understand it, and sometimes because the main focus of all the publications they read is on stock selection. Sure, risk is mentioned, but only in a lip-service way. It is rare indeed to find risk-adjusted returns for stocks, advisory portfolios, or mutual funds.

You may think: "If a mutual fund goes up 15%, then it went up 15%, what difference does the risk-adjusted rate of return make? None!" None in the past—but risk has a way of coming home to roost.

Basic Principle 1

Reduction in portfolio risk can be directly converted into increased return. There is no easier way to increase the return on a portfolio than to reduce its unnecessary risk.

Basic Principle 2

Any individual security should be selected not because it has the highest ratio of expected return to risk over your investment horizon, but rather because it increases the return-to-risk ratio of your entire portfolio more than any other security choice.

1

The concept of risk goes beyond sleeping well: Risk and return are bound together as shown in the box on the previous page.

The first principle emphasizes the close connection between risk and return. That relationship goes beyond the basic concept that higher expected returns carry the burden of higher risk. The second principle is based on a belief in the portfolio view—the emphasis is on building and evaluating your entire portfolio of assets simultaneously, not on an asset-by-asset basis. As this book will show, your portfolio is, indeed, more than the sum of its parts.

Chapter 1 defines risk and focuses on its measurement. The next two chapters examine ways to reduce risk—diversification and asset allocation. Chapter 4 summarizes the relationship between risk and return. Following Chapter 4 is a special section for those who are using AAII's *Stock Superstars Report* advisory service.

There is another approch to risk reduction not addressed here—hedging. Hedging reduces overall risk by being short, or the equivalent, some portion of the portfolio. The most common approaches involve options, which alone require a thick volume (see Bibliography). In addition, the basic concept of hedging is very different from the approaches discussed in this book and needs extensive separate treatment.

The entire book provides the theoretical underpinnings of risk analysis while focusing on practical ways to increase your investment success through risk control.

Chapter

Understanding Risk and How It Is Measured

Individuals invest in different assets in order to receive a return (a profit). Investors may have received this return in the past and expect to receive it in the future. But how dependable is the expected return? Enter the concept of risk.

Risk in general is defined as "the chance of damage, injury, or loss." Investment risk is the chance of loss, but it's not hard to also imagine cases of damage or injury to an investor's well-being as a result of taking on risk. To assess the chance of loss in an investment, it's necessary to refine the definition of risk and try to put it in mathematical terms.

Measuring Risk

Virtually all acceptable measures of risk are based on gauging the dependability of return on an investment. How is dependability measured? Investors look at the volatility of the returns—how much the returns of a security or portfolio vary around the average return. For example, consider two assets A and B as shown in Table 1.1 on page 5.

While the four-year arithmetic average return

for both investments is the same, 10%, you would have more money if you invested in Asset A. The terminal wealth would be $1.46 for every dollar invested as opposed to $1.43 with Asset B, or 2% more. The greater the variation around the arithmetic average return, the more the geometric average will be below the arithmetic average. And terminal wealth is determined by the geometric average. The geometric average is reduced relative to the arithmetic average as a function of volatility. (See A1 in Appendix A for the mathematical formula for geometric average.)

You can see this phenomenon quite easily by considering this situation: If you gain 20% and then lose 20%, you are not even but have lost 4%; if you gain 40% and then lose 40%, you are out 16%. The higher the variation, the more the terminal loss.

Table 1.1 also shows standard deviation, which is the most common measure of return volatility. Standard deviation is calculated as the square root of the average of the deviations from the average, squared (see A2 in Appendix A for the formula).

Why is this calculation used? Simply averaging the deviations from the average would result in some negative numbers and an average difficult to interpret. Looking at the range of returns—simply taking the difference between the two extremes (−0.05 − 0.25 = −0.30, or 0.30)—would not show how tightly other returns were clustered. For example, consider the following two series of returns: −20.0, 0.0, 0.0, 0.0, +20.0 and −20.0, −19.0, 0.0, +19.0, +20.0. They each have the same range, but not the same volatility.

The first series of returns will have 4% higher terminal wealth.

Another measure of volatility that is quite direct is to look at a series of returns and observe the lowest cumulative return over the period under observation. This is called maximum drawdown and is a very common measure in commodities trading. Basically it measures the lowest level an equity reached during a specific period. As with all historical risk measures, maximum drawdown is presumed to be an indication of future risk. It's a useful measure no matter what risk measure is used, but because the drawdown in the future may be greater than in the past, maximum drawdown must be estimated and therefore becomes "expected" maximum

Table 1.1: The Impact of Volatility on Terminal Wealth

	Period Returns (%)				Arithmetic Average (%)	Standard Deviation (%)	Geometric Average (%)	$1 Invested: Terminal Wealth ($)
	1	2	3	4				
Asset A	10.0	10.0	10.0	10.0	10.0	0.00	10.0	1.46
Asset B	25.0	−5.0	5.0	15.0	10.0	11.20	9.4	1.43

Calculating the Averages:

Asset A
Arithmetic Average: $[0.10 + 0.10 + 0.10 + 0.10] \div 4 = 0.10 = 10.0\%$
Geometric Average*: $[(1 + 0.10) \times (1 + 0.10) \times (1 + 0.10) \times (1 + 0.10)]^{1/4} - 1.0 = 0.10 = 10.0\%$
Terminal Wealth of $1: $1 \times [(1 + 0.10) \times (1 + 0.10) \times (1 + 0.10) \times (1 + 0.10)] = \$1.46$

Asset B
Arithmetic Average: $[0.25 - 0.05 + 0.05 + 0.15] \div 4 = 0.10 = 10.0\%$
Geometric Average*: $[(1 + 0.25) \times (1 - 0.05) \times (1 + 0.05) \times (1 + 0.15)]^{1/4} - 1.0 = 0.094 = 9.4\%$
Terminal Wealth of $1: $1 \times [1 + 0.25) \times (1 - 0.05) \times (1 + 0.05) \times (1 + 0.15)] = \$1.43$

*The Geometric Average takes into consideration the compounding effect of the prior period return earning money over the next period. In the equation, ¼ represents the fourth root of the amount in brackets. The fourth root of a number is the amount which, when multiplied by itself four times, results in that number [for example, if $N^{1/4} = R$, then $R \times R \times R \times R = N$].

loss. (The term "expected" is used to mean the best estimate of future return or future risk.) The weakness of historical drawdown is that there is nothing in the measure to indicate the probability of receiving the historical loss, or a greater loss, in the future.

Beta is a very common measure of risk, but it too has its drawbacks. Beta measures the risk of individual assets or portfolios relative to the risk of the stock market as a whole (see A7 in Appendix A for the formula). Market risk is also called systematic risk; it is the volatility all securities face because the overall market has volatility. It cannot be diversified away. (The volatility due to a security's unique characteristics is unsystematic risk, which can be reduced by combining the security with other dissimilar securities.) Beta is simply a measure of how much an asset's returns vary with the variation in the market's returns. Stocks with betas above 1.0 have returns that vary more than the market (have higher systematic risk) and those with returns that vary less than the market have betas of less than 1.0 (have lower systematic risk).

Beta is used less and less because the correlation between stocks seems to be decreasing, making beta less reliable. The validity of beta also depends on efficient market assumptions that are questionable. Finally, it is difficult to establish what a meaningful measure of the total market would be. The S&P 500 index, which is usually used, is really not representative of the entire market—nor is it relevant to the way most individuals invest. For example, very few individuals weight their stock holdings to match the market capitalization of the companies as the S&P 500 does.

Return Distributions

Standard deviation measures volatility on the upside as well as the downside. Clearly, investors don't worry much about their returns being volatile on the upside, although there is an advantage to having some consistency even among positive returns. If the distribution of returns is similar on the upside and downside, both positive and negative returns can be used in estimating volatility. However, examination of historical data shows that the distribution of investment gains and losses is not symmetrical— rather it tends to be stretched out more on one side. This is called skewness and is illustrated in Figure 1.1 (and also discussed further at A3 in Appendix A). Common sense explains the skewness: Losses can only be 100% on the downside (without the use of leverage), but gains can be unlimited on the upside.

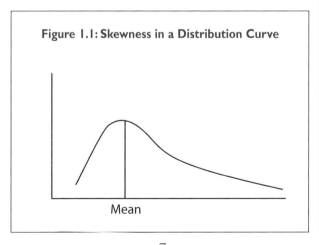

Figure 1.1: Skewness in a Distribution Curve

Mean

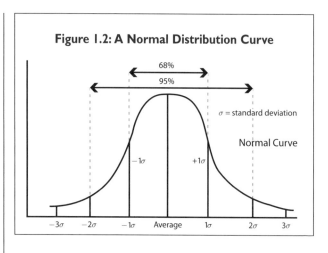

Figure 1.2: A Normal Distribution Curve

σ = standard deviation

Normal Curve

68%
95%

-1σ $+1\sigma$

-3σ -2σ -1σ Average 1σ 2σ 3σ

How do researchers account for skewness in distributions of investment returns? There has been some effort to cope with skewness directly by only measuring the dispersion below the average (see A6 on semi-variance in Appendix A). But the most common way of handling skewness is to ignore it on the basis that within the usual range of returns, skewness disappears. The lognormal curve, which is skewed, is a better estimate of the distribution of stock returns and is used in some models. But the regular normal curve is more commonly used and most estimates of probability you see are based on it. It is shown in Figure 1.2 (see A5 in Appendix A for further explanation of the normal curve).

Another problem with distributions of investment returns is that they tend to be more peaked and have longer tails (kurtosis) than a normal curve (see Figure 1.3 and A4 in Appendix A). While the great majority of observations of return are reasonably close to the average and do form close to a normal (or lognormal) distribution, the true distribution has a significant number of outliers (extreme values). In fact, estimates of the true distribution of returns indicate the possibility that the distribution has infinite variance and standard deviation. This means that the probabilities of loss indicated by the normal curve are not accurate and can be very misleading.

Again, since most of the return distribution is reasonably close to normal, these problems are ignored by most researchers. The assumption of normality in return distributions and the use of standard deviation as the basic measure of risk are almost universal in modern portfolio theory (MPT), which focuses on the relationship between risk and return to construct an optimal portfolio—one with the maximum return for a given level of risk. Further, these assumptions are not only used in assessing portfolio risk directly, but underlie most option evaluation models and the capital asset pricing model (CAPM)—an economic model for valuing stocks that relates

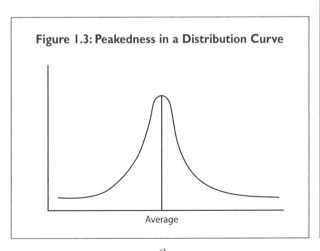

Figure 1.3: Peakedness in a Distribution Curve

Average

risk to expected return.

Though standard deviation and its variations
will be used here, the problems with outliers
should be kept in mind. Several times in
an investment lifetime, market movements
that could occur only once in a million years
according to a normal curve will happen.
Examples of this phenomenon occurred in 1929,
1987, 2000–2002, and 2008.

The failure of Long-Term Capital Management
(LTCM), the hedge fund that made news in
1998, was due in large part to dismissal of
outliers and an excessive use of leverage. LTCM
was based on the many assumptions of modern
portfolio theory, including the assumption of
normalcy. The New York Federal Reserve was
so concerned that the failure of LTCM would
disrupt the U.S. economy that it took the unusual
step of becoming involved in the problem
and convinced a number of U.S. and foreign
institutions to come up with $3.5 billion to save
the fund. (The complete story is told by Roger
Lowenstein in "When Genius Failed: The Rise
and Fall of Long-Term Capital Management";
see Bibliography.)

How can investors use the strong analytic tools
made possible by modern portfolio theory and
not fall victim to outliers? There are several ways.
The worst outlier problems occur with individual
assets—even a large corporation's stock can go
from incredible heights to near zero so quickly
there is no chance to react. The solution here is
diversification—a bit more diversification than
might be called for under a normally distributed

return assumption. Diversification will be covered in Chapter 2.

When the outliers relate to the market as a whole, asset protection is more difficult, but there are several actions that can be taken.

- First, keep a long-term view. While outliers might crush the short-term trader or even the one-year investor, outliers are much less likely to severely damage the returns of those with a three- to five-year horizon.

- Second, while investors can look at the probabilities indicated by the normal distribution in setting risk levels for themselves, this decision can be supplemented with analysis of what has happened historically over different horizons. Since the periods 2000–2002 and 2008–2009 were among the most sustained downturns in recent memory (at least in terms of major averages), investors can evaluate how they have coped and use this in setting risk levels in the future.

- Third, individuals can have some appropriate portion of their portfolio in assets or asset classes that have very low or negative correlations with the general stock market. This approach will be covered extensively in Chapter 3.

Standard Deviation

Volatility measurements tend to be fairly stable

over the long term, but there is wide variation in the shorter term. Because asset adjustment may depend on current volatility, it is important to keep the measurement period short enough to pick up trends, but not so short that it picks up large fluctuations that are momentary. The three-year annualized standard deviation calculated using monthly or weekly periods is a good compromise time frame for making comparisons between stocks, funds and portfolios.

Most U.S. stocks have long-term annual standard deviations of 10% to 100%. The S&P 500 has a long-term annual standard deviation of about 20%. Risk in individual portfolios can be reduced below that of the average stock by diversification (covered in Chapter 2).

Why Investors Are Risk Averse

It is reasonably easy to understand that obtaining successive amounts of additional money, while valuable, is not as valuable to an investor as holding on to what they already have. The general model for this diminishing marginal value of wealth is called utility theory and can be seen in Figure 1.4. Diminishing marginal utility simply means the next increment of wealth added is not worth as much to you as the previous increment.

This concept is particularly true in the area of investment risk and return. As an example, suppose someone offers to flip a fair coin with you. If you lose you must pay X dollars, but if you win he will pay you 2X dollars. You think he is crazy and say OK, but then he says the bet

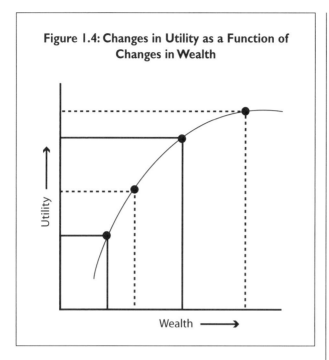

Figure 1.4: Changes in Utility as a Function of Changes in Wealth

Utility

Wealth

is for most of your net worth. A 50% chance of losing all you have for a 50% chance to win twice your net worth is not a rational move for most individuals. You can measure your own decreasing marginal utility of money by following through on the process. Would you gamble two year's income, one year's, or one month's even at two-to-one odds on a 50-50 chance?

Because of decreasing marginal utility, investors are risk averse and are willing to sacrifice some potential return for reduced risk of loss. While this theory, developed by Daniel Bernoulli back in 1738, has been assumed to be true in general, if not in the precise logarithmic exposition he proposed, recent research indicates the theory does not explain real-world investor behavior.

13

Investors may be "loss averse" rather than risk averse. That is, they may be willing to accept risk to avert loss, but not willing to accept risk for a gain. (Please see the Behavioral Finance section at the end of Chapter 4.) And the reduction of risk generally requires some reduction in return, as will be discussed in later chapters.

Chapter

Using Diversification to Control Risk

When discussing portfolio management, the concepts of asset allocation and diversification are often confused because diversification can be used in a general or specific way. Diversification, as we use it, is the choosing of assets within an asset class that are at least partially independent of each other in order to reduce risk. Asset allocation refers to the distribution of investment funds among distinct classes of assets. Asset allocation is not a goal, but rather an approach that attempts to achieve risk reduction, but doesn't always succeed. The ultimate goal of all investors, however, should be reducing risk to the level appropriate for them.

How Assets Are Grouped

Assets that have little or no long-term systematic movement with other assets can be considered a separate class. Chapter 1 introduced the concept of systematic risk, or volatility, as it applies to the stock market. Similarly, bonds and real estate also have their distinct forms of systematic risk.

However, there will be some correlation between asset classes and it will change over time. Correlation coefficients are used to measure

15

how closely a pair of asset classes tends to move in relation to each other. A perfect positive correlation of 1.0 indicates the returns of both classes move up and down at the same time, but not necessarily by the same percentage. The less the correlation between classes, the better the opportunity for effective diversification. A negative correlation means that returns move together, but in opposite directions. Stocks and bonds have had correlations running from –0.3 to 0.6 over the past 70 years, but there is no systematic relationship. Real estate sometimes correlates with the stock market because a strong economy is good for both. Real estate also relates to the bond market because real estate investments are influenced by interest rates. Basically, however, stocks, bonds (debt instruments), and real estate are the three primary asset classes.

What about assets that do not fit into these three groups? There are a wide range of commodities, including precious metals, that can be considered asset classes, but generally these are not assets that generate income. The only profit they generate is from price speculation (although it is often held that they can be effective hedges). However, the stock or bonds of gold mining companies are still stocks and bonds and belong in those asset classes, even though the movement of prices in precious metal mining stocks is correlated to the price of the metal as well as the other aspects of corporate success. But while investing in commodities, fine art, collectibles, etc., can be profitable and provide diversification for risk reduction, these types of investments are not included in the analysis in this book.

The view here is that the distribution of investments between the classes of stocks, bonds, and real estate is asset allocation. Subclasses of asset groups have emerged and are popular in the financial press. For stocks in particular, the subclasses of foreign vs. domestic, small cap vs. large cap, and value vs. growth have become part of the allocation process for some. In such a generalized form this is not only a misleading but also an ineffective approach, as will be discussed more completely in Chapter 3.

Diversification Theory for Stocks

The modern portfolio theory (MPT) approach to diversification begins with the concepts of systematic and unsystematic risk. The very definition of systematic risk, risk resulting from general market action and not from the specific nature of the corporation or its stock, indicates that it cannot be diversified away. Figure 2.1 shows how diversification reduces the risk of a portfolio toward the systematic (market) level.

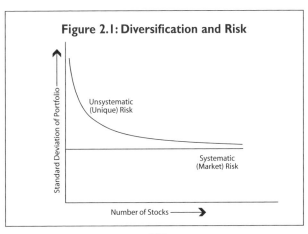

Figure 2.1: Diversification and Risk

Standard Deviation of Portfolio

Unsystematic (Unique) Risk

Systematic (Market) Risk

Number of Stocks

While most stocks have systematic risk, they
do not have the same degree of this risk. While
systematic risk indicates that stocks move with the
market, they do not all move to the same degree
or even in the same direction. As described in
Chapter 1, beta measures the systematic risk of
a stock over a specified period. A beta of 1.0
indicates a stock whose returns vary to the same
degree and direction that market returns vary. A
beta of 1.5 indicates returns one and a half times
as volatile as the market (if the market returns
10%, the stock returns 15% on average). A beta of
0.8 indicates that returns vary only 80% as much
as the market. Beta can be negative, indicating
a stock that moves with the market but in the
opposite direction. A stock with a beta of –1.0
would have a return of –10%, on average, when
the market returns 10%.

Since systematic risk is non-diversifiable,
investors will want higher returns to justify
accepting this risk. Figure 2.2 represents the
security market line (SML), which indicates at
a particular point in time what return can be
expected for accepting a given level of market
risk. Theoretically, in an efficient market all
securities would lie on this line, but occasionally
stocks appear outside the line, as shown by the
two points representing stocks A and B. Clearly,
stock A would be purchased before stocks on the
SML because it provides a higher return for its
level of risk. Just as clearly, stock B should not be
purchased by any rational investor since its return
is lower than its level of risk.

In an efficient market, stocks A and B will
not stay above and below the SML for long. If

MAXIMUM RETURN, MINIMUM RISK: A PRACTICAL APPROACH

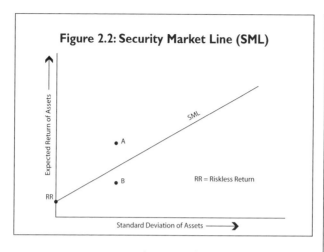

Figure 2.2: Security Market Line (SML)

Expected Return of Assets

SML

• A

• B

RR = Riskless Return

RR

Standard Deviation of Assets

everyone attempts to buy stock A, its price will be driven up (decreasing its expected return) until it resides on the SML. Similarly, stock B will be sold until its price goes down enough to raise its return to the level of the SML. It is important to note that even the least risky stocks may have a level of risk above that desired by an investor. In this case, to lower risk further the individual must go into another asset class.

In order to eliminate most of the unsystematic risk (risk unique to the security), investors must diversify. Any approach to diversification recognizes that a number of stocks must be invested in, but the questions are: how many and which stocks? The naïve approach emphasizes obtaining diversification by increasing the number of stocks. But by simply adding stocks, the investor runs the risk of choosing ones that may have similarities (geography, industry, size) and thus would require more stocks than necessary to achieve an appropriate level of diversification.

19

Based on a large number of studies over the years, the following generalizations can be made:

1) Naïvely diversifying across industries will not provide better diversification than random diversification or choosing stocks without regard to their correlations. This does not preclude reducing risk by diversifying across industries if you choose industries in such a way as to reduce their correlations with each other.

2) Choosing a portfolio of stocks without regard to correlations will likely result in average correlations and a portfolio risk somewhat lower than the risk level of the average single stock. For example, if the average standard deviation of the stocks in your portfolio is 36%, you may be able to achieve a standard deviation of 22% in your portfolio. Most importantly, you can achieve this with about 15 stocks—additional stocks will not help noticeably.

3) Choosing stocks with low correlations to each other and the market can reduce the portfolio risk level even more— perhaps to less than 50% of the average standard deviation of the individual stocks in the portfolio. In this case, a slightly larger portfolio (20 to 30 stocks) will be worthwhile. You can estimate the standard deviation of a portfolio from the historical prices of the stocks in it (see formula A8 in Appendix A). But this formula is quite complex when more than a few stocks are involved.

4) It also appears inconclusive whether diversifying across capitalization size (large, mid, small) reduces risk. The same is true of diversifying across value and growth stocks. The correlation range within each of these subgroups is just as wide as between them. While such style diversification may reduce risk slightly, in a computerized world such a crude approach is like estimating people's weight from their height when there is a scale available. Measure portfolio risk directly, skip the simplistic approaches.

Computerizing the Theoretical Models

The concept of reducing portfolio risk by combining assets that are less than perfectly correlated is now well known. Since no perfect correlations are likely to be found among stocks, portfolios are always less risky than the individual stocks of which they are composed. Combining this with the expected (future estimated) returns of the stocks results in efficient portfolios—those with the maximum return for a given level of risk.

While such analysis was difficult years ago, modern computerized models make theoretical optimization possible. However, making precise estimates of the future returns of all stocks is not very accurate or feasible. In addition, many of the assumptions necessary in these analytic approaches are questionable. Beyond the problem of assuming a normal distribution of returns (discussed in Chapter 1), correlations are not consistent through time—adding significant error to statistical results.

Modern portfolio theory is also hampered by its assumption that we have a highly efficient market. While the market appears to be reasonably efficient, it is not completely efficient for a number of reasons. First, assuming all investors used optimizing approaches in developing portfolios, they would not necessarily make the same estimates of the future risk and return of different equities. Thus, they might derive different valuations and choose different portfolios. Second, investors could all be using the same historical data, but the judgment as to how far back in time to go in making estimates would vary. Third, even if all information relating to every stock is known, the interpretation of this data may vary considerably.

As will be seen in Chapter 3, there are a number of well-established inefficiencies in the market that, together with the problems indicated in Chapter 1, have encouraged researchers to seek market models other than those based on previous modern portfolio theory. Newer models relieve some of the problems, but create problems of their own and so do not help with the goal here of reducing risk through diversification.

While the theoretical work accomplished through the years helps guide investors in the right direction, more practical ways of controlling risk need to be pinpointed. Interestingly, the Nobel Prize was awarded in 2002 for work showing that the assumption of consistent rationality in investors is not always valid, and that markets often are inefficient. Additional studies show that humans depart from the assumed rationality and that "risk averse" may really be "loss averse." For example, an investor might refuse to buy a high-risk stock even with an opportunity for gain. But the same investor will hang on to this stock if he already owns it and take the same risk in order to avoid a loss. (See Kahneman in the Bibliography.)

Low Correlation Is the Key

Any practical attempt at risk reduction through diversification should start with the selection of stocks that are believed to offer superior returns. The various stock-picking approaches that have appeared over the years are not covered here. But the key when using any approach is to avoid choosing stocks whose returns will move together. While, as discussed earlier, random diversification across industries does not provide any more risk reduction than simple diversification, stock-picking approaches that result in choosing most stocks from similar industries will dampen any diversification effect.

One approach you can use with any selection strategy is to simply choose more stocks than you will eventually want. For example, if you want 20 stocks in your portfolio, select 30 to 40 stocks that you think may provide superior returns. Then reduce the number by keeping primarily the stocks with low correlations to the rest of the portfolio.

How do you check stock correlations? One method is to use a spreadsheet such as Excel that contains a correlation function. You can download historical data into the spreadsheet and set up a correlation matrix, as described in

Figure 2.3: Correlation Matrix: 10-Stock Portfolio

Ticker	ARO	AM	AFSI	CVX	ELNK	EBF	GFRE	MDT
Company	Aeropostale	American Greetings Corporation	AmTrust Financial Services	Chevron Corporation	EarthLink	Ennis, Inc.	Gulf Resources, Inc.	Medtronic, Inc.
Industry	Retail (Apparel)	Printing & Publishing	Insurance	Oil & Gas	Computer Services	Office Supplies	Chemical Manufacturing	Medical Equipment & Supplies

Correlation Matrix								
	ARO	AM	AFSI	CVX	ELNK	EBF	GFRE	MDT
ARO	1.000							
AM	0.206	1.000						
AFSI	0.053	0.300	1.000					
CVX	0.005	0.248	0.068	1.000				
ELNK	0.543	0.286	0.137	0.501	1.000			
EBF	0.361	0.494	0.416	0.470	0.605	1.000		
GFRE	0.335	0.108	0.084	0.233	0.076	0.359	1.000	
MDT	0.488	0.136	0.272	0.347	0.519	0.491	0.254	1.000
NOC	0.515	0.307	0.407	0.440	0.624	0.623	0.349	0.718
SYX	0.453	0.275	0.062	0.452	0.439	0.306	0.286	0.441
	ARO	AM	AFSI	CVX	ELNK	EBF	GFRE	MDT

48.2% *Average Standard Deviation of All 10 Stocks*

30.1% *Standard Deviation of Equally Weighted Porfolio of All 10 Stocks*

26.1% *Standard Deviation of Equally Weighted Portfolio of 8 Stocks*
Excludes American Greetings (AM) & Gulf Resources (GFRE)

22.0% *Standard Deviation of Equally Weighted Portfolio of 5 Stocks*
Excludes Aeropostale (ARO), American Greetings (AM), Ennis (EBF), Gulf Resources (GFRE) & Systemax (SYX)

Source: AAII's Stock Investor Pro, Thomson Reuters.

Appendix A under standard deviation (A2). After running the correlation function for all pairs of stocks, you can then choose the low correlation stocks visually. Not only can you vary the stocks selected but you can also weight the stocks with low correlations more heavily (invest more dollars in them). There is simulation software that will search for the lowest risk combination, but given other assumptions this is not really necessary.

The correlation matrix for 10 stocks passing a stock screening strategy is presented in Figure 2.3. As a group, these stocks had a very high standard deviation of 48.2%. However,

NOC	SYX
Northrop Grumman Corp.	Systemax Inc.
Aerospace and Defense	Retail (Catalog & Mail Order)

NOC	SYX

NOC	SYX
1.000	
0.481	1.000

when combined into a portfolio, the standard deviation of the portfolio declines by 38% to 30.1%. The lower risk of the portfolio is the reduction due to diversification.

It can be helpful to start with a larger number of stocks than you want to add to your portfolio and study the correlation matrix or use the solver function of a program such as Excel to minimize risk for given level of expected return. Eliminating two stocks from Figure 2.3 that add the greatest level of risk to the portfolio drops the portfolio standard deviation from 30.1% to 26.1%. A five-stock portfolio can be constructed from the 10 stocks in Figure 2.3 with a standard deviation of 22.0%. This is an example of how adding more stocks doesn't always reduce risk, it actually may add to it. In addition, the weights of the stocks can be changed, rather than investing equally in each one. Increasing the weights of the stocks contributing the least portfolio risk will provide the greatest reduction in risk from diversification.

Excel spreadsheets that perform a wide range of financial, investment and portfolio analysis are presented in AAII's *Computerized Investing* and are available for download from AAII.com.

Chapter 3 reveals practical approaches to putting together a diversified portfolio in conjunction with allocating assets across classes and subclasses.

Combining Stock-Picking Approaches

Instead of selecting a larger number of stocks than is needed and then reducing portfolio risk by choosing the ones with low correlation, an alternative is to combine several different stock-picking strategies or several different advisers' approaches. In either case, the important thing is to make sure the approaches are not essentially the same.

While diversification is generally based on past history on the theory that the relationships that existed in the past will continue to exist in the future, choosing stocks based on different criteria and fundamental approaches will almost guarantee diversification in the future. But the stock selections from different advisers or from different approaches can be checked by analysis using the correlation procedure described above.

AAII uses the combination approach in its Stock Superstars Report (SSR) advisory service. The starting point for the creation of the Stock Superstars Report concept was investment professionals whose approaches have beaten the market over very long time periods. The Stock Superstars Report builds on the work of well-known investors such as Benjamin Graham, William O'Neil, Peter Lynch, John Neff, Martin Zweig, Warren Buffett, David Dremen, John Templeton and others to develop a complete portfolio management system. The system includes monitoring the success of each approach in the current market and utilizing the four approaches that are working best. For more information on the Stock Superstars Report system, visit www.stocksuperstars.com.

Diversifying Within the Real Estate Asset Group

The other major asset classes, bonds and real estate, also require diversification. In the case of real estate, the ability to diversify effectively with individual assets is severely limited. Individual real estate assets are extremely expensive and even partnership shares are generally limited to qualified investors (high net worth or income) who invest over $100,000. Even with several million dollars, diversification across different types of real estate and different geographical regions would be difficult.

One solution is to invest in REITs (real estate investment trusts). REITs are very similar to mutual funds except they invest in real estate enterprises, primarily the ownership, renting and managing of properties. Investors can find REITs involved in every area of real estate. The major subclasses of equity REITs, and their percentage of all equity REITs, are:

- Industrial/Office 26%,
- Retail 23%,
- Residential 15%,
- Health Care 11%
- Diversified 9%,
- Lodging/Resort 9%, and
- Other 7%.

Mortgage REITs are closer to debt instruments than real estate and should be considered a subgroup of the bond asset class.

REITs cannot invest in short-term speculation or development. Individuals who choose to invest in these aggressive areas must do so through a limited partnership, which would not have the mutual fund characteristics of a REIT. Every limited partnership is unique and without continuous pricing, correlations cannot be made with other real estate investments or with other asset classes.

Information about REITs, including performance data, can be found at the NAREIT website (www.reit.com) (see References). REITs can be analyzed for diversification in the same way as stocks by performing your own correlation analysis.

Another way to diversify is to purchase one of the mutual funds that invest in a wide range of REITs. The Vanguard REIT Index fund (VGSIX) is one example, and it is used in Chapter 3 as a stand-in for the REIT asset class. Other fund families also have REIT mutual funds. The Vanguard REIT Index fund is based on the Morgan Stanley REIT index and is capitalization-weighted. There are also REIT exchange-traded funds (ETFs) such as iShares Cohen & Steers Realty Majors Index fund (ICF). Although REITs are not evaluated here in terms of market capitalization (share price times number of shares outstanding), the comments about indexes in Chapter 3 might well apply. In any event, investors will need a method of choosing the best REITs, before looking at correlations, when selecting the REITs themselves.

Diversifying Within the Bond Asset Group

For the purposes of this book, the bond asset group includes all debt instruments, bonds, bank accounts, CDs, money market funds, etc.

Although the terms systematic and unsystematic risk are not used when discussing bonds, they do have diversifiable and non-diversifiable risk. The risk that is common to the entire bond market is interest rate risk. All bonds are affected by interest rate changes and generally in the same direction. However, as with stocks, not all bonds will be affected to the same degree. Generally, the longer the maturity date or the higher the duration (an alternate bond maturity measure that considers the present value of remaining payments, not just time), the greater will be the impact of an interest rate change. However, inflation and expected interest rate changes can alter the impact.

Since longer maturities usually provide both higher returns and greater risk within the same default risk segment, the normal economic risk/return pattern of rewarding greater non-diversifiable risk applies to bonds. It is possible to diversify across maturities: Building a portfolio with a range of maturity dates is called creating a ladder. The main use of investment-grade bonds should be controlling risk in a portfolio made up largely of higher return assets. Under this scenario, there is little reason to own anything but short-term bonds. However, there are certainly exceptions: Individuals may want to eliminate virtually all risk, or they may be satisfied with the returns they can receive from bonds and don't want to bother with the effort required to increase their returns.

The above does not apply to individuals who invest in higher risk or junk bonds. The high-yield bond group is a completely different area of investing; in many ways it is similar to investing in stocks since corporate profits are an important aspect of analysis. The analysis is a little more specialized because firms with high-yield bonds are generally not profitable. With high-yield bonds, default risk becomes a major concern. This is the risk that you will not receive your principal or your promised interest.

There is some default risk in all bonds, except U.S. government bonds and bonds guaranteed by the government. It is because of default risk that diversification of bond holdings becomes desirable. Unfortunately, there is no historical data from which to derive correlation tables and thus diversification becomes naïve. The riskiness of bonds is not determined by ordinary statistical analysis of returns. Bonds have limited life and by the time volatility, beyond interest rate volatility, showed up it would be too late for action. Default risk in bonds is based on ratings given by three agencies (Fitch, Moody's, and Standard & Poor's). And while there are eight to 13 rating categories, they can be reduced to three basic grades: investment grade, speculative, and default. In the case of municipal (tax-free) bonds, insurance is also available on many issues. Ratings are based on estimates of the issuer's ability to repay, which is based on financial strength.

Because bonds trade most efficiently (low transaction costs) in large blocks, often $100,000, a great deal of diversification is not practical for the vast majority of individuals. Most investors will find using a mutual fund or an ETF or investing in government bonds the most efficient way to diversify. Those who invest in speculative or default bonds must find a way to diversify that avoids the default risk that is tied to a single factor such as industry problems, changes in the law, or regulatory issues that might affect all of one's holdings simultaneously.

Diversification Increases Returns

Effective diversification is the first line of defense in controlling and reducing risk. And the reduction of risk not only protects us from investment disaster but, as will be shown in Chapter 4, allows us to increase our returns by minimizing the percentage of assets we will need in low-return, protective assets.

MAXIMUM RETURN, MINIMUM RISK: A PRACTICAL APPROACH

Chapter

Combining Diversification With Asset Allocation

Asset allocation became a popular investment topic in recent years based on a mistaken interpretation of a research study. A published work showed that over 90% of the variation in investment returns was associated with asset allocation. But those quoting the research reported that over 90% of returns are determined by asset allocation as opposed to individual asset selection. The study said nothing about the impact on the level of returns, but this misinterpretation spawned a flurry of articles and Web pages devoted to asset allocation strategies.

Asset Allocation Usually Ignores the Destination

While they all take the same general approach, common asset allocation approaches disagree strongly on the details. The general approach is to mandate that at a certain age, you should have a certain percentage of your wealth in each of stocks, bonds, cash, and sometimes other asset classes such as real estate. Often, they further divide each class into subclasses. For example, stocks might be divided into: large vs. small, domestic vs. foreign, or value vs. growth. The approaches will then briefly mention that this reduces risk, but there will be no analysis of how it does this or proof that it works. The emphasis will be on the debate over whether a 50-year-old should have 50%, 60%, or 70% in equities.

Most of these writings treat the topic as if asset allocation were an end in itself, rather than one possible tool in the creation of a portfolio that provides the highest return for a given level of risk. This is akin to arguing about the best road to take before you decide where it is you want to go.

Readers of a certain age will remember Adele Davis, the famous nutritionist. When she would lecture, invariably she would be asked something like, "Are tomatoes good for me?" Her response would be, "Which tomatoes, grown where?" Similarly, the response to a writer advocating a certain percentage in bonds vs. stocks should be "Which bonds, which stocks?"

Take a portfolio that is 70% invested in an S&P 500 index fund and 30% in a bond index fund, and calculate its risk. Invariably, you could find a different 100% stock portfolio that is less risky than the 70%/30% indexed portfolio, and you could also find a 100% bond portfolio that is more risky.

Allocation may be helpful, but the key to risk control is the selection of the individual assets in the portfolio. Diversification within asset classes is more important than the allocation between classes because asset allocation is used only to eliminate risk that cannot be reduced by diversification—and almost always at a reduction in the rate of return. Choose individual investments first, allocate weightings later.

More Problems With Traditional Allocation Approaches

In addition to this general problem of mistaken emphasis, there are some special problems with the usual approach to asset allocation. These include:

- Stocks and bonds sometimes move in the same direction, sometimes in opposite directions, and sometimes independently. Any allocation between them must adjust to this reality.

- Foreign stocks in a portfolio may reduce short-term risk, but this effect dissipates over a few years as economic conditions travel. And if, as in 2008, the economic downturn is worldwide, U.S. equities and the equities of other developed countries will move together. Emerging market stocks or the stocks of any smaller group of countries may move based on unique circumstances.

- Pigeonholing all stocks into either value or growth doesn't make sense. Fifteen percent of all stocks are truly value stocks, 15% are truly growth stocks if determined by momentum, and 70% are "something else." If you allocate between a value index fund and a growth index fund, you are primarily investing in "something else" stocks, which may not have the risk-reducing effect you want.

- In any approach to controlling risk, investment horizon and risk aversion should be important factors. The use of age as a surrogate for investment horizon is too simplified. Some people retire at 62, while many others work into their 80s. Many individuals do not plan on using up all assets during retirement, but want to pass their wealth on to heirs. So the level of risk any investor should assume at any point in time depends on factors more complex than age.

- The allocation of wealth across stocks of companies of different sizes as a method of controlling risk has its limitations. Typically, the size of a stock is measured in terms of market capitalization (share price times number of shares outstanding), and classified as micro, small, medium or large. Since over the long run micro-cap stocks outperform other stocks, particularly large caps, it may make more sense to look for portfolio diversification within the small-cap, micro-cap and perhaps mid-cap markets. For individuals who use mutual funds, there is a real danger of over-investing in large-capitalization stocks and of not being adequately diversified because most funds weight their holdings based on market capitalizations (the larger the company, the more of the stock in the index). An S&P 500 index fund will have 19% of its assets invested in the largest 10 stocks. Not only is this too much concentration, but the largest stocks often have high correlations. So, you may think you are getting diversification, but you aren't. While it may come as a surprise, the S&P 500 index is not a very well-diversified portfolio, nor are most indexes.

Allocation between certain asset classes can be a tool to reduce risk. However, simplistic approaches should be set aside in order to look at all the factors that influence the risk of a portfolio. And, most importantly, the nature of the individual assets in each class must be considered before deciding on the allocation between classes. For example, you might choose to allocate a different percentage of assets to an equity portfolio with a standard deviation of 11% than one with a standard deviation of 14%.

As previously discussed, only stocks, bonds, and real estate can be considered unique asset classes for our purposes. Limited partnerships are treated as stocks. For convenience, stocks can be divided into first-level subclasses by capitalization size and value versus growth. Bonds can be divided into short term (which includes bank accounts and CDs) and longer term. We use three years as the short-term limit.

Implementing the Popular Approach

Here's how the popular approach typically works. Table 3.1 presents a list of major asset classes and subclasses (using index mutual funds and ETFs as surrogates), with their long-term (eight-year) average returns and their three-year average risk level as measured through their standard deviation. The eight-year time period was chosen because most individuals have longer-term holding periods, and the eight-year returns

37

Table 3.1: Return of Asset Classes

Asset Class	Mutual Fund or ETF Surrogate (Ticker)	Standard Deviation (Last 3 Yrs) (%)	8-Yr Avg Annual Return (%)	Portfolio Standard Deviation of 14.1%	
				Asset/T-Bill Ratio (%)*	Asset/T-Bill Return (%)**
U.S. Total Stock Market	VTSMX	22.9	7.7	62/38	5.6
Large-Cap Stocks	VFINX	22.2	6.6	64/36	5.0
Equal-Weight Large Caps	VADDX	27.2	9.8	52/48	6.1
Large-Cap Growth	VIGRX	22.5	6.9	63/37	5.1
Large-Cap Value	VIVAX	22.9	7.2	62/38	5.3
Small-Cap Stocks	IWM	28.0	10.7	50/50	6.4
Small-Cap Growth	IWO	28.1	10.8	50/50	6.5
Small-Cap Value	IWN	28.7	10.3	49/51	6.1
Micro-Cap Stocks	DFSCX	29.2	11.3	48/52	6.5
Foreign Stocks	VGTSX	28.5	11.8	49/51	6.9
REITs	VGSIX	40.0	11.2	35/65	5.3
Gold Stocks	VGPMX	42.5	21.8	33/67	8.6
Total Bond Market	VBMFX	4.3	4.9	330/-230	11.3†
Cash (90-Day T-Bills)	T-Bills	0††	2.1	—	—

Percentage invested in asset and percentage invested in T-bills to produce a portfolio with a standard deviation of 14.1%.
**Return from asset/T-bill portfolio with a standard deviation of 14.1%.*
† For a portfolio with a standard deviation of 14.1%, bonds are leveraged by borrowing at the risk-free rate and the portfolio return is increased.
†† On a daily basis, T-bills have some risk, but assuming a 90-day holding period there is no risk.

Data as of December 31, 2010.

are an excellent estimate of long-term future returns since it appears to include a full market cycle.

Table 3.1 also shows what percentage of each asset class could be combined with Treasury bills to achieve a certain level of risk, in this instance a portfolio standard deviation of 14.1%—which, at the time of this writing, was the current risk level of the widely touted allocation 60% stocks/40% bonds. For example, a portfolio consisting of 64% large-cap stocks and 36% Treasury bills would achieve a portfolio standard deviation of 14.1%. Table 3.2 looks at some sample asset allocations and provides each portfolio's standard deviation and expected return (based on the long-term historical return). The first two examples are typical recommendations among the major asset classes, and the second two examples are typical recommendations that include subclasses.

How do these portfolios stack up? In Table 3.1 the asset class with the highest return is gold stocks at 21.8%, and that class combined with T-bills provides the highest return, 8.6%, while keeping the portfolio standard deviation at 14.1%. The bond class indicates a higher return if you could leverage by borrowing at 2.1%. In most cases it would be difficult to borrow at less

Table 3.2: Sample Asset Allocations

Portfolio*	Standard Deviation (%)	Return** (%)
Portfolio 1: 60% Stocks/40% Bonds	14.1†	6.6
Portfolio 2: 80% Stocks/20% Bonds	18.5	7.1
Portfolio 3: see below	15.9	6.9
Portfolio 4: see below	18.0	7.2

Allocations	Portfolio 3	Portfolio 4
Large-Cap Growth	20.0%	20%
Large-Cap Value	20.0%	20%
Small-Cap Growth	12.5%	10%
Small-Cap Value	12.5%	10%
Bonds	25.0%	20%
Cash	10.0%	10%
REITs	0.0%	10%

*Surrogates used in this table are the same as those used in Table 1; for Portfolios 1 and 2, stocks are all U.S. stocks (represented by VTSMX) and bonds are all bonds (represented by VBMFX).
**Based on 8-year historical average annual return.
†Standard deviation of 14.1% used for normalization in Table 3.1.

Data as of December 31, 2010.

than the 4.9% yield, so leveraging is not feasible; therefore, gold stocks and T-bills remain the highest-yielding combination with a portfolio standard deviation of 14.1%. There are two important considerations here. First, it is possible for a well-chosen portfolio to have a higher return and/or a lower risk than the general class to which it belongs. So the data here is an approximation of possibilities. Second, it would not be wise to have only one class in addition to T-bills in a portfolio because risk and return in one class can change rapidly. For example in the last edition of this book (2005), gold stocks had the second-poorest return (foreign stocks had the poorest return) and the second-highest risk (small-cap growth had the highest risk).

In Table 3.2 you can see the risk and return results of several combination portfolios that are often suggested.

The Alternative: Build From the Bottom

There is no question that allocation across asset classes may reduce risk but we don't know by how much until we know which investments in each class are involved. What we want is to add holdings to our portfolio that, in our estimation, have good prospects for superior returns and have low correlations with the other holdings. Which particular class those assets belong to is not the important issue.

A more effective approach to controlling risk is to start from the bottom and find investments with the potential for good returns, and then to choose a portfolio from among those investments. The objective, once again, is to get the highest return within an acceptable level of risk. To control risk (unless you have a very high risk tolerance), it will probably be necessary to have some assets that are not equities or are a very different form of equity, such as real estate investment trusts (REITs).

Another weakness in the traditional asset allocation approach is that the returns and risk levels of the benchmarks are averages for asset classes (Tables 3.1 and Table 3.2). Well-chosen portfolios—portfolios in which the individual securities that are selected have good return prospects and low return correlations—will have much better return/risk ratios than portfolios with securities that are the average in each asset class.

In addition, almost all the indexes and mutual funds used as asset class benchmarks consist of portfolios that are capitalization-weighted—a greater percentage of the portfolio is invested in companies with larger market capitalizations. As previously pointed out, smaller-cap stocks outperform larger-cap stocks, so the same index stocks and portfolios would perform better if equally weighted. In fact, an investor throwing darts at a sheet of listed stocks, selecting 30, and investing an equal amount in each one would have an incredibly good chance of beating the S&P 500 by a significant margin over the long run. You can see the impact of cap weighting by comparing VADDX (equally weighted large caps) and VFINX (cap-weighted large caps) in Table 3.1.

The Problem With Traditional Rebalancing

What about changing allocations over time? The traditional approach would be that if the accepted allocation was 60% stocks and 40% bonds and the stock market ran up, you would need to sell stocks and buy bonds to maintain the original percentage allocation. Once again, the problem here is that the approach is losing sight of the true objective—to control risk. Perhaps selling stocks and buying more bonds when the market goes up is a good idea sometimes. But, maybe not.

Imagine that the U.S. moves into a bull market after several years of weakness. The first year would likely be very strong for stocks, and conventional wisdom would dictate readjusting the stock/bond mix. But what if—and it is not unlikely—because stocks are moving up with some consistency, their risk is going down, and with the economy starting to perk up and the Federal Reserve doing its thing, bonds are becoming more volatile (risky)? This scenario may be unfolding as this is being written in early 2011.

The alternative rebalancing approach is to maintain your given risk level. And to maintain the risk level you have chosen, you might find you should actually be buying stocks and selling bonds as stocks go up. With portfolio management websites and software or other sources of volatility information, you can monitor the risk of your portfolio on a continual basis and make adjustments as needed.

One word of caution: Regardless of the approach to rebalancing, don't do it too often. Annually is more than enough. Not only are transaction costs and perhaps taxes involved, but there is strong evidence of short-term serial correlation. In other words, assets going up tend to keep going up—at least in the short term.

Once again, artificial percentages that hope to control risk are silly in the computerized age when risk can be dealt with directly and diversification can be obtained by adjusting the assets in the portfolio using correlations. As you can see, conventional asset allocation is an effort to achieve diversification by dividing the individual investments among various asset classes and subclasses in the hope, sometimes misguided, that a mix will achieve efficient diversification. On the other hand, diversification is the effort to divide our investments among individual securities that have low correlations with each other and thus reduce risk.

Fundamental Concepts to Risk Reduction

Before starting to design a portfolio that addresses your risk/return needs in a practical way, it is important to understand some major concepts that underlie any approach.

1. Volatility Affects Returns

The variability of the return on a portfolio's assets, which is the accepted definition of risk, affects not only the "sleep well" aspects of the portfolio, but also the real return. This was

43

pointed out at the beginning of Chapter 1 and is the result of volatility reducing the geometric return, which is the determinant of terminal wealth.

2. Diversification Affects Returns

While effective diversification within the same asset class will reduce risk, it may reduce return as well. This is because not all potential investments have the same likelihood of gain. If you didn't care about risk, you would put all of your assets into the single investment you thought had the likelihood of the greatest gain. But in order to diversify, you must put some assets in investments that you expect will have less potential return. At the same time, however, you anticipate that the reduced risk will be worth the reduced gain. Trying to reduce risk while giving up as little return as possible is the critical part of the strategy suggested in this book, which will be emphasized in Chapter 4.

3. Cap-Weighting Affects Returns

Although the risk and return data of the indexes of various asset classes is used as a surrogate for the risk and return of the various classes themselves, portfolios chosen by astute investors from these asset classes, as previously pointed out, should have higher returns and lower risk than the indexes themselves. On the other hand, if you use mutual funds instead of individual stocks, the risk and return may be closer to the indexes, since many mutual funds cap-weight their portfolios.

In addition, the larger-capitalization stocks tend not to be value stocks, yet value stocks, as defined by their lower price-to-book ratios (stock price per share divided by book value per share), outperform growth stocks over the long run. As an example of this effect, over the last eight years the S&P 500 index has had an average annual return (through December 31, 2010) of 6.6%. However, the return of the S&P 500 unweighted by market capitalization (in other words, the average stock in the S&P 500) was 9.8% a year. This is the return the average dart thrower would have received on stocks. And to throw in another shocker: From the beginning of 2000 through the middle of 2002, the NASDAQ composite index was down 80%—a drop from which it has not fully recovered as of early 2011—but this was an up market for the average NASDAQ stock. The average stock was up 50% a year during the period. The bear market existed only for a few hundred technology stocks, but their capitalization weight dominates the other 3,000 stocks in the NASDAQ index. You can monitor this difference at the Wilshire website at no charge (www.wilshire.com, click on Indexes, then Index Return Calculator). This is why the dart thrower should outperform the indexes and a thoughtful individual should outperform the dart thrower.

Note, too, that the risk in the weighted indexes is increased because the stocks that are most heavily weighted tend to be correlated, and thus diversification among these larger stocks has less impact. Small- and micro-cap indexes also are capitalization-weighted, and equally weighted individual stock portfolios chosen from these asset subclasses will have lower risks than the indexes.

Table 3.3 shows correlations among the various indexes. Numbers approaching 1.0 indicate greater correlation in return performance; negative correlations indicate that returns tend to move inversely: When one index has a positive return, the other tends to be down. Whatever the risk and return levels of the indexes used, you can expect that your portfolio, if not cap-weighted, will have a lower risk and a higher return.

How can you develop a portfolio that establishes a risk level suitable for you and offers the highest returns while maintaining that level of risk?

There are two steps:

• Establish a risk level you can live with, and

Table 3.3 Correlation of Asset Classes (Based on Eight-Year Return

Index (Ticker)	Asset Class	U.S. Tot Stk Market	Large Caps	Eq-Wt Large Caps	Large-Cap Grth	Large-Cap Value
VTSMX	U.S. Tot Stk Market	1.00	1.00	0.98	0.97	0.97
VFINX	Large Caps	1.00	1.00	0.97	0.97	0.98
VADDX	Equal-Wgt Large Caps	0.98	0.97	1.00	0.95	0.95
VIGRX	Large-Cap Growth	0.97	0.97	0.95	1.00	0.89
VIVAX	Large-Cap Value	0.97	0.98	0.95	0.89	1.00
IWN	Small Caps	0.94	0.92	0.95	0.91	0.89
IWO	Small-Cap Growth	0.93	0.90	0.93	0.92	0.85
IWN	Small-Cap Value	0.93	0.91	0.94	0.87	0.91
DFSCX	Micro Caps	0.93	0.90	0.94	0.89	0.88
VGTSX	Foreign Stocks	0.91	0.91	0.89	0.87	0.90
VGSIX	REITs	0.77	0.76	0.80	0.71	0.77
VGPMX	Gold Stocks	0.71	0.69	0.71	0.70	0.67
VBMFX	Total Bond Market	0.05	0.07	0.06	0.00	0.12
	Cash*	-0.02	-0.01	-0.06	-0.02	0.00

*90-day T-bills.
Data as of December 31, 2010.

- Choose the individual assets and asset classes that will provide the highest return within that risk level. Table 3.3, along with Table 3.4, which shows asset class returns and volatility, can provide some guidance.

Setting a Suitable Risk Level for Yourself

There are a number of ways you can approach setting a suitable risk level. By looking at the standard deviation of returns for different classes and using the normal curve, you can establish the percentage chance of losing different portions of your assets during a particular time period. Those probabilities can be seen in the Appendix A discussion of the normal curve (A5). [A similar approach, in the context of mutual fund investing, was described in an article that originally appeared in the *AAII Journal* and is reprinted in Appendix B.] However, the

Small Caps	Small-Cap Grth	Small-Cap Value	Micro Caps	Foreign Stocks	REITs	Gold Stocks	Total Bond Market	Cash*
0.94	0.93	0.93	0.93	0.91	0.77	0.71	0.05	-0.02
0.92	0.90	0.91	0.90	0.91	0.76	0.69	0.07	-0.01
0.95	0.93	0.94	0.94	0.89	0.80	0.71	0.06	-0.06
0.91	0.92	0.87	0.89	0.87	0.71	0.70	0.00	-0.02
0.89	0.85	0.91	0.88	0.90	0.77	0.67	0.12	0.00
1.00	0.99	0.98	0.99	0.82	0.79	0.67	-0.03	-0.06
0.99	1.00	0.94	0.98	0.82	0.73	0.69	-0.05	-0.06
0.98	0.94	1.00	0.98	0.80	0.83	0.63	0.00	-0.06
0.99	0.98	0.98	1.00	0.81	0.78	0.64	-0.04	-0.08
0.82	0.82	0.80	0.81	1.00	0.69	0.82	0.15	0.03
0.79	0.73	0.83	0.78	0.69	1.00	0.56	0.18	-0.04
0.67	0.69	0.63	0.64	0.82	0.56	1.00	0.18	0.03
-0.03	-0.05	0.00	-0.04	0.15	0.18	0.18	1.00	-0.04
-0.06	-0.06	-0.06	-0.08	0.03	-0.04	0.03	-0.04	1.00

Table 3.4: Asset Class Return and Volatility

Asset Class	Mutual Fund	Ticker
U.S. Total Stock Market	Vanguard Total Stock Mkt Idx Inv	VTSMX
Large Caps	Vanguard 500 Index Investor	VFINX
Equal-Weight Large Caps	Invesco Equally-Wtd S&P 500 Y	VADDX
Large-Cap Growth	Vanguard Growth Index Inv	VIGRX
Large-Cap Value	Vanguard Value Index Inv	VIVAX
Small Caps	iShares Russell 2000 Index	IWM
Small-Cap Growth	iShares Russell 2000 Growth Index	IWO
Small-Cap Value	iShares Russell 2000 Value Index	IWN
Micro Caps	DFA US Micro Cap I	DFSCX
Foreign Stocks	Vanguard Total Intl Stock Index Inv	VGTSX
REITs	Vanguard REIT Index Inv	VGSIX
Gold Stocks	Vanguard Precious Metals and Mining Inv	VGPMX
Total Bond Market	Vanguard Total Bond Market Index Inv	VBMFX
Cash	90-Day T-Bills	

Data as of December 31, 2010.

following is a shorter approach that is more intuitive and avoids the problem of outliers when using a normal curve for the distribution of investment returns (as explained in Chapter 1).

The first assumption is that you are a long-term investor: If your holding period is less than three years, you should not be in stocks, but in low-risk debt instruments. Examining the history of the stock market since World War II can help you judge your reaction to losing periods. Since 1946, what is the worst that could have happened to your portfolio if all you held was the S&P 500 index?

During the 1973–1974 period (based on calendar years), you would have lost 37.4% of your investment in the S&P 500. The three-year period of 2000–2002 had a loss of approximately 43%, and in 2008 the loss ran to 37%. In all

3-Year		8-Year	
Annual Return (%)	Standard Deviation (%)	Annual Return (%)	Standard Deviation (%)
(1.7)	22.9	7.7	15.7
(2.9)	22.2	6.6	15.2
1.7	27.2	9.8	18.5
(0.6)	22.5	6.9	15.4
(4.4)	22.9	7.2	16.0
2.3	28.0	10.7	20.5
2.2	28.1	10.8	21.1
2.2	28.7	10.3	20.5
2.1	29.2	11.3	21.4
(5.3)	28.5	11.8	19.8
1.5	40.0	11.2	27.5
2.2	42.5	21.8	31.5
5.8	4.3	4.9	3.9
0.6	0.2	2.1	0.5

cases, the loss indicated is based on buying at the beginning of the year. This is generally not the case since investors usually buy stocks over time and the actual loss would be less or no real loss at all. But people tend to look at the highest level their portfolio reached and measure loss from that point—at least from the highest year end.

For the purposes of assessing risk preferences, the 2000–2002 and the 2008 down periods are of benefit. When discussing risk in past periods, investors tend to say they would have ridden it through because they know it turned out all right. But the S&P 500 could go down again. Did you ride through these downturns or did you reduce your equity holdings, indicating your portfolio risk was inappropriately high? Nothing will give you more guidance about your risk tolerance level than an honest appraisal of your feelings and portfolio actions during the 2000–2002 and 2008 periods.

Assume the S&P 500 will have several periods of a 40% drop during your investment lifetime. The S&P has a long-term annual standard deviation of about 20%, so this should provide an indication of what standard deviation you are willing to assume. Contemplating occasional losses in the range of 40% and knowing how you

49

felt during this past year should enable you to set an appropriate risk level. For example:

- If you can face a roughly 40% drop every 10 to 20 years and believe that in the long run stocks will prosper, you don't need to be in any asset class outside of U.S. stocks, although you will still want to diversify to keep your risk as low as possible while obtaining the long-term high return of stocks. (This does not include your short-term cash reserves as part of your investment portfolio.)

- If, on the other hand, you can only face a maximum of a 20% loss, you will need a portfolio with a standard deviation of about 9%. It will be difficult to reduce risk to this level or lower without moving a significant portion out of stocks.

Assume for this discussion that you want to keep portfolio decreases under 30%, which implies a portfolio standard deviation below 14%. You may recall from the earlier discussion and Tables 3.1 and 3.2 that an allocation of 60% stocks/40% bonds would not quite keep risk below this level (it would have a standard deviation of 14.1%) if we used the existing indexes of those two asset classes. You would have to go to a 55% stock/45% bond allocation. However the standard deviations of the past three years are much higher than their long-term averages. Table 3.4 provides annual standard deviations of the asset classes over the last eight years. And those figures might be better for future decisions.

You may notice that the probabilities discussed do not match the probabilities that would be derived from a normal curve. We have used history to adjust the tails of the return distribution. In short, outliers (extreme values) exist. They shouldn't be assumed away.

You should be able to beat the 60% stock/40% bond portfolio return with the same level of risk because, as discussed, selected portfolios in the various asset classes will usually outperform cap-weighted indexes.

Getting the Highest Return at a Given Risk Level

Once you have selected an appropriate level of risk, the next step is to create a portfolio that provides the highest return for that risk. Of course no one knows what the future holds, so the selection of individual assets must be based on your own estimates. But the information here should give you some idea of which classes and subclasses you should examine. In studying the data in Tables 3.3 and 3.4, remember that results for the past eight years are somewhat different than those over the past 50 years, and the three years 2008–2010 have been very atypical. The correlations in Table 3.3 are close to those for the very long run even though there may be short-term variations.

How might you create your own portfolio? On paper, you will usually get the best return at a given risk level by combining the highest return asset class with the safest class in the proportion that gives you the desired risk level. For instance, looking at Table 3.1, if this were eight years ago, you could have selected a portfolio consisting of 33% gold stocks and 67% T-bills, maintained your portfolio standard deviation at 14.1% and had a compound return close to 8.6% a year. That combination would not have done well for the last three years when the best would have been pure bonds. In the last edition of this book five years ago, REITs would have been the best primary investment.

It would have been hard to predict that result in advance, however, and asset class returns can change in a hurry. Even if you monitor your portfolio closely and adjust frequently, things can change too quickly to be invested in only one equity subclass. Remember how quickly energy stocks collapsed and tech stocks before that?

So how do you go about selecting which classes to be in? The first clue is the correlation between classes as shown in Table 3.3. The only negative correlations with the stock classes are in the bond classes. So to reduce risk significantly, there will need to be debt issues which includes cash (money markets, T-bills, CDs) in your portfolio. The percentage you put in debt depends on what else you choose.

If your investment horizon is three years or longer, short-term government bonds have no risk and can be used instead of cash and provide a higher return. As explained in Chapter 2, there is no reason for individual investors to own long-term bonds in a balanced portfolio.

In selecting which other asset classes to invest

in, look at those that have had the highest returns in the very long run, with additional weight given to those also doing well in the short term. From the top classes look at the correlations and try to choose those with low correlations to each other. This is not a pure numbers game, nor is there one best way because the returns of each class for the future are not known.

With the standard deviations of each class and the correlation coefficients given in Tables 3.3 and 3.4, you can determine the standard deviation of any combination of asset classes in a portfolio. The standard deviation of the portfolio is a function of the standard deviations of each class, the fractional weight given each class and the correlations between each pair of classes. This is the same procedure as for individual assets. Further details are provided in Appendix A (A8).

Based on the preferences and biases of this book, the following is a more direct approach:

- Eliminate bonds, except for short-term bonds.

- Based on results from over the last 70 years, from this year, and from all long-term periods in between, eliminate all stocks on the S&P 500 index—along with any total stock market index fund (there are now some equally weighted indexes and these might be a possibility). If you are screening for individual stocks, you can simply eliminate stocks with over $2 billion market capitalization. This preference for smaller stocks is based primarily on very-long-term returns, but there are also some intuitive reasons to avoid giant companies. These include the hundreds of professionals analyzing these stocks, and the fact that high-speed trading and other institutional gambits can only take place in high-volume stocks or indexes.

- The correlation between foreign and U.S. stocks is too great for there to be meaningful long-term diversification, and over the long term the returns have been lower. This eliminates foreign stocks. While emerging market stocks are foreign, we consider them a separate class with historically above-average returns and therefore they may be suitable for investors who understand them.

- Over the long term, there is not much to engender excitement for gold mining stocks, even though the correlations with other asset classes are low and they have had a great period of high returns. However, a small holding in mining stocks is not unreasonable.

- Categories not listed that may be suitable include mid-cap stocks. Mid-cap value stocks have a return similar to small-cap value. Also, you can include any value stock with a capitalization of less than $2 billion in your choices.

Beyond a bond portion, the suggested portfolio make up is REITs, small-cap and mid-cap value stocks, and micro-cap stocks.

However, it would be wrong to suggest that equity investments in other categories are never successful. There are excellent investments in other categories; they are just not as common. Why look for gold in a well-worked mine when new veins exist elsewhere? But if you come across any outstanding opportunity—take it.

How do you define the stock size and style categories? There are no consensus definitions, but the Glossary at the back of this book provides recommendations.

One caution: When selecting value stocks, choose a real measure of value rather than the classification that splits all stocks into either growth or value. One criterion would be that the price-to-book ratio must be below 1.5, and lower—perhaps 1.0—is better.

In terms of the percentages to invest in each category, invest an approximately equal amount in each, and then after examining the risk of such a portfolio, invest enough in short-term bonds to reduce the risk level to one appropriate for you.

For example, an initial stock portion of the portfolio could be:

28% micro cap (value or growth)
28% small-cap value
28% mid-cap value
16% REITs

Remember from previous discussion that the best portfolio might come from only one or two of these classes.

How do you choose the specific investments within each class? The methods of choosing a pool of potential stocks in each asset class have been the subject of thousands of books. You can design your own approach or you can rely on the advice of others. The process of diversifying the individual issues within each class was the subject of Chapter 2. The degree to which you are able to diversify and allocate among equity subclasses will reduce the percentage of low-return, safe investments you will have to add to the portfolio to maintain your required risk level.

One effective approach, discussed in Chapter 2, is to select more stocks in an asset class than you actually want. You can then set up a correlation matrix based on historical prices and choose those with the lowest correlations with each other.

You should review the entire portfolio after you finish choosing individual investments in each class. Say you have four asset subclasses (not including your bond portfolio) and have selected 10 stocks in each of them. You can once again set up a correlation matrix and see if all of the individual issues are necessary. You may well find that many of the individual stocks are highly correlated even if they are in different subclasses and you can eliminate the ones you feel will produce the lowest returns.

If you prefer investing in mutual funds, there is no reason not to include funds that invest in the asset classes you need. However, as previously discussed, keep in mind that index funds and large-cap funds that are almost like index funds are ineffective. You can treat a fund just as a stock in setting up an effective portfolio and analyzing its risk. Some large-cap funds that use a different approach and are not "me too" funds might be included. ETFs are frequently a better choice than traditional mutual funds.

Once a suitable portfolio has been established, it is necessary to monitor and adjust it. With three or four equity asset subclasses, it will not be necessary to check risk levels constantly and, in fact, short-term variations should be ignored. If the risk of your portfolio starts to increase and continues to increase over a month or more, you should look at the components, see where the additional risk is coming from and make adjustments as necessary. While we are not discussing ways to choose stocks or asset classes, the approach used for doing this must also be monitored. Real estate, for example, has had long bull runs at times and even though it is an excellent hedge (low correlation) for other equities, REITs may not always have the returns reflected in Table 3.4. In fact, 1998, 2008, and 2009 were very poor years.

Monitoring can be done by looking at the components of your portfolio, or by looking at the risk levels of the fund surrogates listed in Tables 3.3 and 3.4. The risk of securities and surrogate funds can be found at Morningstar.com (see References) or other analytic sites. The annual AAII Guide to the Top Mutual Funds and separate Guide to ETFs provide risk comparisons for funds and indexes.

Chapter

The Risk/Return Relationship

The introduction to this book laid out two basic principles that underlie any intelligent approach to investing. They are:

Basic Principle 1

Reduction in portfolio risk can be directly converted into increased return. There is no easier way to increase the return on a portfolio than to reduce its unnecessary risk.

Basic Principle 2

Any individual security should be selected not because it has the highest ratio of expected return to risk over your investment horizon, but rather because it increases the return-to-risk ratio of your entire portfolio more than any other security choice.

These principles are the foundation of the conviction that investing must have a portfolio orientation. The investment portfolio is more than the sum of its parts. The best overall returns for the individual investor may well come from a portfolio consisting of stocks with expected future returns lower than could have been selected. This chapter explains the importance of the portfolio approach and shows why it is better than simply going for the highest expected return stocks.

The Long-Term Impact of Lower Volatility

In Chapter 1, Table 1.1 illustrated that even though two assets may have equal arithmetic average returns, if one has a lower volatility (standard deviation), it will have a higher geometric average return and thus a higher terminal wealth. Table 4.1 goes a step further in this example.

As can be seen, Portfolio A with a lower average annual return has a higher geometric average return and terminal wealth than Portfolio B. This is due to the reduction in volatility (risk). Therefore, reducing risk directly increases the true rate of return (the geometric average).

Reducing Stock Risk Changes Asset Allocation

Chapter 3 illustrated that in order to maintain risk at an acceptable level for most investors, some quantity of bonds would have to be included in

Table 4.1: The Impact of Lower Volatility

	Period Return (%)					
	1	2	3	4	5	6
Portfolio A	10.0	10.0	10.0	10.0	10.0	10.0
Portfolio B	2.0	20.0	−6.0	28.0	−11.0	33.0

Terminal Wealth:

$$(1 + R_1)(1 + R_2)(1 + R_3)(1 + R_4)(1 + R_5)(1 + R_6)$$

Portfolio A:

$$(1.1)(1.1)(1.1)(1.1)(1.1)(1.1) = 1.77$$

Portfolio B:

$$(1.02)(1.20)(0.94)(1.28)(0.89)(1.33) = 1.74$$

Arithmetic Average (%)	Geometric Average (%)	Standard Deviation (%)	Terminal Wealth* ($)
10.0	10.0	0.0	177,000
11.0	9.7	16.9	174,000

*$100,000 invested at the beginning of period 1.

the portfolio's asset allocation (Table 3.1). This is because bonds are the only assets with very low or negative correlations to the various stock subclasses (Table 3.3). Because the return on bonds—particularly short-term bonds, which are most effective—is low compared to stock classes, there has to be a trade-off of return for risk reduction. It follows then that the lower the risk of the stock part of the portfolio, the lower the proportion of the portfolio that will have to be in bonds, and the higher the average return. Therefore, reducing the risk of the stock portion of the portfolio will directly translate into higher returns for the overall portfolio.

While this risk/return relationship is obviously true for typical investors who have some of their portfolio in low-return safe assets, it is also true for the aggressive investor. In the case of aggressive investors who are completely in stocks, reducing the risk of the stock portfolio would permit them to use margin (borrowing money to buy additional shares) and still maintain their desired level of risk. This would increase returns, assuming the returns are higher than the margin interest.

Effective diversification can reduce unnecessary risk, often with little effort. It should be apparent why Principle 1 is important to understand. An attitude of "find the best returns and risk will take care of itself" wastes the opportunity to increase returns.

Trading Return for Risk Reduction

When should you trade return for risk reduction? The ultimate opportunity is when you can no longer get rid of unnecessary risk and must accept the lower returns of safe bonds to bring your overall portfolio to the risk level you desire.

There are other times for trade-offs within the selection process of your stock portfolio. Since risk reduction can be converted to additional return, you are really looking at choices that involve accepting a lower return at one point to get a higher return at another. Table 4.1 illustrates the end product of this process. Assume the stocks in Portfolio A were chosen even though they had a lower expected return (10% versus 11%) than those in Portfolio B, and that these are historical results. A higher expected return was sacrificed when choosing the stocks in order to reduce portfolio risk. This choice translated into a gain in return that was higher than the expected return sacrificed.

What is the process by which this trade-off might occur? It follows the multiple asset

Table 4.2: The Risk/Return Trade-Off

	Expected Return (%)	Standard Deviation (%)	Return-to-Risk Ratio	Correlation With Stock A
Stock A	20.0	30.0	0.67	1.00
Stock B	18.0	20.0	0.90	0.70
Stock C	17.0	20.0	0.85	0.30
Portfolio AB	19.0	23.1	0.82	
Portfolio AC	18.5	20.4	0.90	

model as shown in A8 in Appendix A; Table 4.2 illustrates a simple example using two stocks.

Assume you have purchased Stock A for your portfolio and must now choose between Stock B and Stock C. Stock B has a higher expected return. It also has a higher ratio of return to risk than Stock C, 0.90 (18%/20%) as opposed to 0.85 (17%/20%). Based on the return-to-risk ratio, you would choose Stock B if you were making a decision in isolation. But you want to see the impact of adding Stock B or Stock C to a portfolio containing Stock A.

The second half of Table 4.2 shows the returns and standard deviations for equally weighted portfolios AB and AC. The return-to-risk ratio is 0.90 for Portfolio AC and 0.82 for Portfolio AB. Therefore, Stock C is the better choice. This illustrates Principle 2.

Why does the higher return-to-risk ratio make it the better choice? If a standard deviation of 20.4% is your preferred risk level, you could buy Portfolio AC and have a return of 18.5%. To maintain a risk level of 20.4% while investing in Portfolio AB, you could only have 91% of your funds in this portfolio; the rest, 9%, would have to be in riskless securities returning an estimated 3.5%. This would result in a total return of 17.6% [(91% × 19%) + (9% × 3.5%)]—not as good as Portfolio AC at 18.5%.

Even if you wanted to accept more risk, you would receive a higher return by leveraging Portfolio AC with the use of margin to the level of risk you wanted. The overall return would be higher at any level of risk compared to investing in Portfolio AB. Why is this true? The lower correlation of Stock C with Stock A makes all the difference. And the impact of lower correlations becomes even stronger as the number of stocks involved increases.

You can now understand why all the media emphasis on specific stocks is distressing. When listening to experts answer questions about different stocks from callers on CNBC, you will sometimes hear them ask about the individual's risk situation, but you never hear anyone ask, "What other stocks are in your portfolio?" And, as this book has shown, that is the critical question.

This portfolio approach cannot be emphasized enough. If you were the manager or coach of a sports team, how do you decide which players to use in the game? The highest paid, the most famous, or the ones who will win more games and championships because of their contribution to the team's performance? Investing is a team sport and each individual security has to be measured not on some individual statistic, but on how it contributes to the portfolio's success.

No one knows for sure how any individual stock will perform, not even over the long run. But multiple stocks selected by rational criteria and then filtered through an analysis of how they interact with each other provides a portfolio that will, over any reasonable term, provide positive returns in excess of the returns of any of the popular indexes.

In an ideal long-term portfolio, it is likely that one or more assets will be performing poorly. This does not necessarily mean that they were poor choices. They may be providing diversification and be the superior performers when the economy changes in the next quarter.

Behavioral Finance

At various places, this book has alluded to problems with various assumptions of modern portfolio theory and its underlying assumptions— rational investor behavior and the efficient market hypothesis. There is a growing body of evidence that:

1) The decreasing marginal utility of wealth is not the best explanation of observed risk aversion;

2) The behavior of individual and, in some cases, institutional investors is not rational in the accepted sense;

65

3) The market is less efficient than efficient market hypothesis postulates; and

4) Much of modern portfolio theory rests on weak assumptions.

While it is not possible to go into all of this here, there are several books in the Bibliography (see Kahneman, Taleb, and Shleifer) that do so very well. What is important to point out is that concern with risk and the use of diversification is critical to investment success even if the current process of measuring risk and correlation is flawed.

The "outlier" problem and the question of distribution shapes were discussed and because of weaknesses in current methodology emphasis was given to looking at historical equity performance and adjusting for worst-case scenarios.

The one area of behavioral finance that is disturbing is the strong evidence that investors are less than rational in their decision making. Without strong determination, emotion will win over reason. All of the rules of efficient portfolio management will be useless if they are not followed.

Supplement for SSR Users

The *Stock Superstars Report* (*SSR*) is a portfolio-oriented, common stock information source. It is published by the American Association of Individual Investors (AAII) and delivered via website, email, a telephone hotline, and print mailing. If you are not currently a subscriber, please log on to our website at www.stocksuperstars.com for a full description.

The purpose of this supplement is to help *SSR* subscribers integrate the concepts of this book with the use of the *SSR* information source. To a great degree, the *SSR* emphasizes portfolio formation as well as individual stock selection and integrates these concepts following the principles described in Chapter 4. Consequently, *SSR* subscribers who form portfolios of 36 stocks benefit from the risk reduction that has already been done.

However, subscribers who have decided to maintain a portfolio of fewer than the 36 stocks should apply the principles of this book to their stock selection process. A minimum of 16 stocks is strongly advised, and 20 to 24 is preferable—based on the risk-reducing impact of diversification. Holding 24 stocks will come close to the diversification effect of holding 36.

The basis for deciding how many stocks to hold relates to minimizing transaction costs. There are two components of transaction costs—

commissions and the spread between the bid and ask prices. These components operate in the opposite direction from each other. The greater the number of shares in each trade, the lower will be the commission as a percent of the acquisition or sale. On the other hand, if you are buying or selling a substantial amount of stock in a single trade, you will impact the spread and have to pay more for purchases and receive less for sales. You can work out the trade-off from experience and make your decision. In any event, hold at least 16 stocks and use a deep-discount broker to minimize trading costs.

How do you decide which stocks to invest in initially for your portfolio? And then, what process should you use to manage your portfolio? The sections below provide some guidance.

First-Time Portfolio Construction

First, and most important, divide the number of stocks across the *SSR* groupings as evenly as possible. This will eliminate much searching for low correlations. Within each category, it is generally best to choose the most recent portfolio additions because the criteria used for both return and risk selection is freshest. However, a few weeks is not going to make a great deal of difference on average.

Assume you decide on a portfolio of 16 stocks, four stocks from each group. You would take the most recent additions to the portfolio from each group and you could further analyze them for minimum risk. You can set up a correlation table as described in Chapter 2. If the risk contribution of all stocks is almost even, you can eliminate the oldest portfolio additions, or make your selections using other personal criteria. This procedure was illustrated in Chapter 2 (Figure 2.3).

Ongoing Selection

When a stock you own is eliminated from the portfolio, you must replace it. You can either replace the stock immediately or wait for the new information from *SSR*. You can choose a new stock from the portfolio that you don't own, including the most recent portfolio additions. However, when examining the stocks you do not own for a replacement, be sure to choose one from the same group.

The above procedures should enable you to achieve almost all of the benefits of the *SSR* approach even if you have fewer stocks. Again, 16 stocks is the recommended minimum; move to the full 36 stocks as soon as practical.

Appendix A

A1: Arithmetic Average, Geometric Average, and Terminal Wealth

The arithmetic average is what we generally think of as the average. It can be calculated in Excel using the AVERAGE function. The formula for the average (mean) return from a series of returns is:

$$r_{AA} = \frac{1}{n}\sum_{i=1}^{n} r_i = [r_1 + r_2 ... r_n] \div n$$

where r_i = return for period i

The geometric average (mean) is reduced relative to the arithmetic average as a function of volatility. It can be calculated in Excel using the GEOMEAN function. The formula for geometric average is:

$$r_{GA} = \sqrt[n]{(1+r_1)(1+r_2)...(1+r_n)} - 1$$

Terminal wealth is determined by the geometric average. It can be calculated by using the GEOMEAN function of Excel, adding 1 and then raising it to the nth power. The formula for terminal wealth is:

$$\text{Terminal Wealth} = (1+r_{GA})^n$$

or

$$\text{Terminal Wealth} = (1+r_1)(1+r_2)...(1+r_n)$$

In the range of returns most commonly used, the following approximation is useful:

$$\frac{\text{Geometric}}{\text{Average Return}} = \frac{\text{Arithmetic}}{\text{Average Return}} - \frac{\text{Standard Deviation}^2}{2}$$

Using numbers from Table 4.1 (Portfolio B) on pages 62-63:

$$= \quad 0.110 \quad - \quad \frac{0.169^2}{2}$$

$$= \quad 0.110 \quad - \quad \frac{0.029}{2}$$

$$= \quad 0.110 \quad - \quad 0.015$$

$$= \quad 0.095 \text{ or } 9.5\%$$

A2: Standard Deviation

Standard deviation is calculated as the square root of the average of the deviations from the arithmetic average, squared. The standard deviation of a security's rates of return has the formula:

$$\sigma = \sqrt{\frac{\sum_{i=1}^{n}\left(r_i - r_{AA}\right)^2}{n}}$$

r_i = return for period i

r_{AA} = arithmetic average return

To calculate standard deviation using Excel, use the STDEV function. The Yahoo! website (finance.yahoo.com) can be used to obtain necessary data. Get an extended quote for any security or mutual fund. Choose Historical Prices. Set up for monthly prices if using two or more years. Set up for weekly prices if using one year or less. Choose download, and prices will be placed in an Excel spreadsheet. Since these are prices, you'll need to calculate returns with the formula "= ending price/beginning price – 1" using the closing price in each row. You can then use this column of returns in the STDEV formula. The standard deviation must be adjusted to put it in the usual annual form. If you used monthly data, multiply by 3.464; if weekly data was used, multiply by 7.21. These figures are the square root of the number of periods in a year.

A3: Skewness

Skewness is the tendency for a distribution curve to be stretched out more on one side (asymmetrical), as shown below. The skewness can be in either direction, but in security returns the tail would be to the right. When the lognormal curve is used, skewness becomes slight.

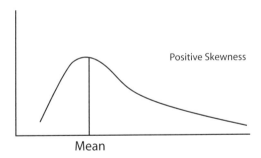

Positive Skewness

Mean

A4: Peakedness (Kurtosis)

This is a measure of how peaked a distribution is beyond that of a normal curve. Security returns are peaked as illustrated:

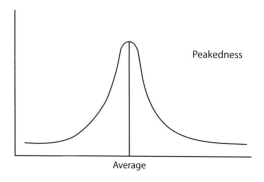

A5: Normal Distribution Curve

The normal distribution curve, as illustrated, can be described by only two measures, mean and standard deviation. We know the percentage of the distribution that is within any number of standard deviations.

- 68% of returns fall within one standard deviation on each side of the average. There's a 32% chance of returns falling outside this range and a 16% chance of returns falling on any one side.

- 95% of returns fall within two standard deviations on each side of the average. There's a 5% chance of returns falling outside this range and a 2.5% chance of returns falling on any one side.

- 99.7% of returns fall within three standard

deviations on each side of the average. There's a 0.3% chance of returns falling outside this range and a 0.15% chance of returns falling on any one side.

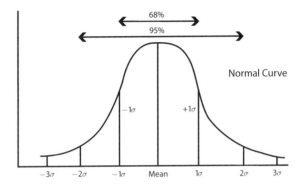

A6: Semi-Variance

Semi-variance is a measure of volatility that only measures returns below the average. While it makes intuitive sense, results will be very close to variance (variance is standard deviation squared) and the semi–standard deviation will be very close on a relative basis to standard deviation. The formula is the same as in A2, but only uses the returns (r) below the average (r_{AA}) and n is the number of returns used.

$$\sigma = \sqrt{\frac{\sum_{i=1}^{n}\left(r_i - r_{AA}\right)^2}{n}}$$

r_i = return for period i
r_{AA} = arithmetic average return
where ($r_i - r_{AA}$) for all $r_i \leq 0$

A7: Beta

Beta, as generally used, is the slope of the regression line between the returns over time of an individual security and an index of the entire market. The formula is:

$$B = \frac{\text{cov}(r_m, r_s)}{\text{var } m} = \frac{\sum\limits_{i=1}^{n}(r_{mi} - r_{ma})(r_{si} - r_{sa})}{\sigma_m^2}$$

r_{mi} = market rates of return

r_{si} = security rates of return

r_{ma}, r_{sa} = arithmetic average of the market return and security return

A8: Standard Deviation of a Portfolio

The portfolio standard deviation can be determined most easily by using the period rates of return of the portfolio and applying the regular standard deviation formula (A2). However, there may not be a history of portfolio returns. In that case, the standard deviation of the portfolio can be determined by the standard deviations of the individual securities, the correlations between them, and the weight of each security in the portfolio, using the following formula:

$$\sigma_{port} = \sum_{i=1}^{n} w_i^2 \sigma_i^2 + \sum_{i=1}^{n}\sum_{j=1}^{n} w_i w_j r_{ij} \sigma_i \sigma_j$$

w_i = proportion of portfolio in asset i

r_{ij} = coefficient of correlation i, j

The calculations are quite extensive if many securities are involved. A more practical way of carrying out such an analysis would be to follow the spreadsheet procedure outlined in A2 for calculating the standard deviation of one security. As described in A2, download the historical prices into Excel from Yahoo! and calculate the returns for each period from the prices. Do the same for each security and then put the return data for each stock in adjacent columns. Create a new column that is the average of the returns for each period. Then use STDEV to calculate the standard deviation for the portfolio. Remember to convert to an annual basis, as in A2. If the securities have different weights, the average column should be a weighted average. This can be accomplished by weighting each return with the proportion of dollars in each asset. The sum of the weights must equal 1.0.

Appendix B

How do you set a suitable risk level for yourself? One way is to establish a worst-case scenario—the percentage loss that would occur if diversification failed and all of your assets went down simultaneously.

Your own risk level is whatever percentage loss you could withstand without abandoning your portfolio positions. In an article that appeared in the AAII Journal, *John Markese discussed the approach in the context of mutual fund investing, and it is reprinted here. This approach can easily be adapted for those building their own portfolio.*

Financial Check-Up: Figuring Out Your Mutual Fund Portfolio

By John Markese, Vice Chairman of AAII

Here is an approach and a simple worksheet that will help you get a grip around all your funds as a portfolio. It will give you insights into your funds individually and force you to assess whether the funds you own make sense when they are taken together as a portfolio.

The Framework

The worksheet in Table 1 provides you with a framework to evaluate expected risk and return for individual funds and your portfolio of funds. There are some assumptions built into this approach that are important. First, the annual

Table 1: Worksheet for Mutual Fund Portfolios

Fund Category	A Portfolio Weight (%)	B Annual Yield* (%)	C Annual Capital Gain* (%)	D Downside Risk** (%)
Money Market	_____	4	0	0
Bond, General	_____	6	0	10
Corporate	_____	6	0	10
Government	_____	5	0	10
High-Yield Corporate	_____	10	0	30
Stock, General	_____	1	10	40
Large Stock	_____	2	8	40
Small Stock	_____	0	12	50
Growth Stock	_____	0	11	50
Value Stock	_____	3	8	40
Sector	_____	0 to 6	4 to 14	20 to 70
International	_____	2	10	50
Emerging Markets	_____	0	14	70
Total	100%			

Average Portfolio Yield = Add A × B for each fund category

Average Portfolio Capital Gain = Add A × C for each fund category

Total Return = Average yield plus average capital gain

Downside Risk = Add A × D for each specific fund category

*Long-term average annual compound yield and capital gains estimates assume reinvestments of income; significant annual variation can be expected for categories and individual funds.
**Annual decline potential based on severe bear market conditions and the conservative assumption that all fund categories would decline simultaneously.

yield and annual capital gains percentages for the fund categories are long-term averages that can vary year-to-year but are historically reasonable. The longer your investment period, the more likely you are to experience similar returns.

Can your individual fund performances differ from these averages? Yes—and the differences can be significant. The more diversified your fund, however, the more likely that it will be similar to the average. However, the more funds trade securities, incurring transaction costs, and the greater the expense ratio, the more likely that funds will underperform these numbers. And it is important to note that these returns are before taxes, so the less tax-efficient your fund is, the lower your aftertax returns will be.

In other words, index funds will be closer to these long-term averages, and actively managed individual funds will have performance distributed both above and below these numbers. But it is important to remember that these are only informed guesses, and future performance may well differ from history and will certainly do so in the short run. If you feel the need to adjust any of these figures, particularly the stock fund numbers, err on the conservative side, reducing the capital gains component. These numbers would probably be 1% to 2% lower if the experience of the 1990s were completely removed. Also, dividend yields have dropped dramatically over the same period, and these expected annual yield figures are near all-time lows. And if your mutual fund is not an index fund with naturally low expenses (expenses are netted out against income) the yields will be even lower.

Risk: The Downside

The downside risk measure is a practical look at what might happen to the value of your mutual fund portfolio in a worst-case scenario.

What is a worst case? That would occur if diversification among different fund categories fails and all of your funds fall in unison. The downside percentage loss in value in any one year for the mutual fund categories is based on post–World War II experiences for average funds. Are there plenty of funds that have done worse in any year? Yes, but they again tend to deviate significantly from these norms when they are not as broadly diversified as the category average.

Taking a look at the amount by which your mutual fund portfolio could drop in a year will give you a feeling for just how appropriate your fund portfolio risk level is relative to your risk tolerance. Converting the percentage downside potential of the funds to dollars, which will be explained, is the test of your ability to sustain short-term losses without breaking your long-term financial plan (selling off investments at absolutely the wrong time, after a market drop).

Fund categories are listed in the worksheet, and general entries are made for money market, bond, and stock funds. Under the bond and stock fund general categories, there are breakdowns of fund types that cover almost all funds.

Municipal bond funds are not a separate listing, but adjusting yields for long-term government bond funds or money market funds for taxes (1.00 minus your federal tax rate in decimal form times the government bond or money market yield) will give you a useful approximation.

Money market funds and short-term government bond funds have yields that are close enough for planning purposes, and the yields on intermediate-term bond funds are equally close to long-term bond funds. Capital gains for money market funds are zero because of their structure. Capital gains for bond funds are shown to be zero under the assumption that over the long term, the impact of interest rate changes and economic cycles will net out capital gains and losses to zero. Clearly, actual holding periods, particularly short-term ones, could produce significant capital gains or losses—primarily for long-term bond funds with average maturities of bonds in the portfolio over 10 years.

Under the stock category, both stock size—large and small—and investment approach—growth and value—are separately listed.

Small stocks are riskier than large stocks, and a growth approach is riskier than a value approach. But the surprise is that value stocks tend to have about the same returns in the long run as growth stocks, although the growth approach beat value for most of the last decade of the 20th century. Probably the highest historical returns, but not the highest risk, have been in portfolios holding small value stocks. If you are not quite certain where a stock fund fits, but you are sure it is diversified, just think of the general stock category as an appropriate match. And if you have a balanced fund, one that holds both stocks and bonds, 50% in each for example, half would be general bond and half general stock.

Sector funds are all over the board as the name indicates, but only very concentrated, high-risk funds, such as in technology or biotechnology, would approach a 14% long-term capital gain average, which would be paired with a 0% yield. An average utility stock sector fund might be close to a 4% yield and a 6% capital gain, as an illustration of how to use the sector figures. The downside risk for the biotech fund or technology sector fund is 70%, for the utility fund, 20%. The higher the yield, the lower the capital gains, and the less the downside risk; conversely, the lower the yield, the higher the capital gains, and the greater the downside risk.

International stock funds are affected by currency exchange risk and are inherently risky, even when investing in large international companies that are indistinguishable from large domestic companies. Emerging market funds, however, have greater currency risks but also significant risk from government instability and less diversified economies. Funds that hold stock from many emerging markets are clearly less risky than single-country or regional emerging market funds.

How It Works

Time for an example. Example 1 shows how you can use the worksheet by plugging in your mutual fund portfolio and doing some simple arithmetic. The portfolio weight percentage is the market value of a fund divided by the total market value of all funds in your portfolio. If you have financial investments other than mutual funds and want to use this approach for your entire portfolio, take the market value of each investment—stock, bond, or fund—and divide it by the total market value of all financial

Example 1: An Aggressive Portfolio

Fund Category	Portfolio Weight (%)	Annual Yield (%)	Annual Capital Gain (%)	Downside Risk (%)
Money Market	10	4	0	0
Bond, General	____	6	0	10
Corporate	____	6	0	10
Government	____	5	0	10
High-Yield Corporate	____	10	0	30
Stock, General	____	1	10	40
Large Stock	30	2	8	40
Small Stock	30	0	12	50
Growth Stock	____	0	11	50
Value Stock	____	3	8	40
Sector	____	0 to 6	4 to 14	20 to 70
International	25	2	10	50
Emerging Markets	5	0	14	70
Total	100%			

Average Portfolio Yield = 1.5% = $(0.10 \times 4) + (0.30 \times 2) + (0.30 \times 0) + (0.25 \times 2) + (0.05 \times 0)$

Average Portfolio Capital Gain = 9.2% = $(0.10 \times 0) + (0.30 \times 8) + (0.30 \times 12) + (0.25 \times 10) + (0.05 \times 14)$

Total Return = 10.7% = 1.50% + 9.20%

Downside Risk = 43.0% = $(0.10 \times 0) + (0.30 \times 40) + (0.30 \times 50) + (0.25 \times 50) + (0.05 \times 70)$

investments in your portfolio. Then fit your non-fund investments into an appropriate category. Here, the example assumes only mutual fund investments and represents an aggressive portfolio mix appropriate for investors with long horizons, low cash needs, and a strong tolerance for short-term downside moves in their total portfolio.

In Example 1, yield is relatively low, at 1.5%, and it should be reinvested if income is not required. Mutual fund shares, however, can always be redeemed to provide cash. The capital gains, at 9.2%, are substantial, and compounded

Example 2: A Conservative Portfolio

Fund Category	Portfolio Weight (%)	Annual Yield (%)	Annual Capital Gain (%)	Downside Risk (%)
Money Market	10	4	0	0
Bond, General	____	6	0	10
Corporate	____	6	0	10
Government	30	5	0	10
High-Yield Corporate	10	10	0	30
Stock, General	____	1	10	40
Large Stock	____	2	8	40
Small Stock	____	0	12	50
Growth Stock	____	0	11	50
Value Stock	40	3	8	40
Sector (Utility)	10	4	6	20
International	____	2	10	50
Emerging Markets	____	0	14	70
Total	100%			

Average Portfolio Yield = 4.5% = (0.10 × 4) + (0.30 × 5) + (0.10 × 10) + (0.40 × 3) + (0.10 × 4)

Average Portfolio Capital Gain = 3.8% = (0.10 × 0) + (0.30 × 0) + (0.10 × 0) + (0.40 × 8) + (0.10 × 6)

Total Return = 8.3% = 4.5% + 3.8%

Downside Risk = 24.0% = (0.10 × 0) + (0.30 × 10) + (0.10 × 30) + (0.40 × 40) + (0.10 × 20)

over long periods will create substantial wealth. The short-term cost of this long-term wealth accumulation is portfolio volatility—this aggressive portfolio may decline by 43% in value in a single year. That means that if you have $1 million invested, you may have a potential unrealized loss of $430,000. The question you must ask is whether you can sustain this kind of loss without breaking your long-term plan. If not, reduce the total commitment to stocks across the board, eliminate high-risk investments such as emerging markets, and increase investments in money market funds, or bond funds with shorter average maturities.

At the other extreme is Example 2, a very conservative portfolio, perhaps for someone in retirement. The stock/fixed-income breakdown is 50%/50%, and the stock fund portion is decidedly income-oriented. The 40% in value stock funds could conceivably be in an index fund, in separate large-cap and small-cap funds, one broadly diversified value fund, or some combination. The 10% in a utility sector fund would be somewhat redundant if the value funds had significant positions in utility stocks.

The bond portion of the portfolio is primarily in a government bond fund. An average maturity for this fund in the seven- to 10-year range would capture almost all the return of the longer maturity bonds while avoiding some of the volatility of the longest sector of the yield curve. The 10% in the corporate high-yield (junk) category is a pure income boost supported by a diversified holding in junk bonds, which spreads default risk over a large portfolio base. And while the downside of the high-yield category is three times that of the government bond fund category, it is still less than the growth stock category.

Notice in Example 2, as compared to the aggressive portfolio in Example 1, that yield (income) is up, capital gains are down, and total return is down. But downside risk is nearly halved, at 24% for this portfolio. The trade-off: lower return for higher income, and lower growth for lower risk.

Note, however, that if the stock component drops much below 50%, the growth—capital gains—that can be generated by this portfolio starts to fall below most expectations of the long-term inflation rate experience of 3% to 4%, eroding the real value of the portfolio over time. The capital gains rate for this conservative portfolio falls within the long-term inflation range by generating a 3.8% growth rate.

Running the Numbers

The worksheet is designed to "put up" your portfolio and see what it may generate over time in terms of income, return, and risk. It also allows you to move the mix around and observe the trade-offs. When you multiply the downside percentage against your portfolio value, you can test your financial courage.

A side benefit of running your portfolio through this worksheet is that it forces you to categorize your investments, and to evaluate whether your portfolio is redundant, has gaps, is concentrated, diversified, rational versus your goals, or just a big cumulative, historical mess.

And while you're at it, count the number of funds you have. If the number of fund choices under your control (not in 401(k) or 403(b) plans) is out of control (eight is typically enough), it's probably time to clean house.

Glossary

arithmetic average: see A1 in Appendix A.

ask price: price a seller is willing to accept for the security; also called the offer price.

asset allocation: the distribution of investment funds among distinct classes of assets, such as stocks, bonds and real estate.

beta: a measure of a stock's risk relative to the market, usually the Standard & Poor's 500 index. The market's beta is always 1.0; a beta higher than 1.0 indicates that, on average, when the market rises, the stock will rise to a greater extent and when the market falls, the stock will fall to a greater extent. A beta lower than 1.0 indicates that, on average, the stock will move to a lesser extent than the market. The higher the beta, the greater the risk. (See A7 in Appendix A.)

bid price: price a buyer is willing to pay for a security.

capital asset pricing model (CAPM): an economic model for valuing stocks that relates risk to expected return.

capitalization-weighted: weighting the holdings of a fund or index based on market capitalizations (larger companies take a larger position in the portfolio).

correlation: the relationship between two assets. Correlation coefficients are used to measure how closely a pair of asset classes tends to move in relation to each other. A perfect positive correlation of 1.0 indicates identical fluctuations—both classes tend to move up and down at the same time by similar amounts. The lower the correlation, the better the diversification; −1.0 means perfect negative correlation.

diversification: the process of accumulating securities in different investments, types of industries, risk categories, and companies in order to reduce the potential harm of loss from any one investment.

geometric average: see A1 in Appendix A.

growth stocks: stocks of companies with rapid and expanding growth (momentum stocks) or stocks that are not value stocks.

index fund: a mutual fund whose portfolio is designed to track a particular market index.

junk bond: bond purchased for speculative purposes; usually rated BB and lower and has a high default risk.

large-cap stocks: stocks with market capitalizations over $2 billion.

long-term bonds: bonds with a weighted-average maturity of greater than 10 years. The longer the maturity, the greater the change in value when interest rates change. Longer-term bonds are riskier than shorter-term bonds and they usually offer higher yields.

marginal utility: general model for the diminishing value of wealth, in which the next increment of wealth added is not worth as much to you as the previous increment.

market capitalization: number of common stock shares outstanding times share price. Provides a measure of firm size.

micro-cap stocks: stocks with market capitalizations under $150 million.

mid-cap stocks: stocks with market capitalizations between $500 million and $2 billion.

modern portfolio theory (MPT): strategy that focuses on the relationship between risk and return to construct an optimal portfolio—one with the maximum return for a given level of risk.

REIT: real estate investment trust; similar to mutual funds except they invest in real estate enterprises, primarily the ownership, renting and managing of properties.

return-to-risk ratio: return of a security or portfolio divided by its risk (standard deviation).

risk: possibility that an investment's actual return will be different than expected; includes the possibility of losing some or all of the original investment. Measured by variability of historical returns or dispersion of historical returns around their average return.

S&P 500 index: broad-based, market-cap weighted index based on the average performance of approximately 500 widely held common stocks.

semi-variance: see A6 in Appendix A.

Sharpe ratio: rate of return of an asset minus

the risk-free rate of return divided by standard deviation.

short-term bonds: bonds with a weighted-average maturity of less than three years.

skewness: see A3 in Appendix A.

small-cap stocks: stocks with market capitalizations between $150 million and $500 million.

standard deviation: a measure of the degree to which returns of an asset vary around the mean. (See A2 in Appendix A.)

systematic risk: the volatility all securities face that cannot be diversified away; market risk.

unsystematic risk: volatility due to a security's unique characteristics that can be reduced by combining the security with other dissimilar securities.

value stocks: stocks of companies whose price looks cheap relative to earnings, assets, dividends or cash flow.

Wilshire 5000 index: a broad-based, cap-weighted index of stocks. Includes virtually all liquid securities (over 5,000).

Bibliography & References

Books and Articles

AAII's Shadow Stock Portfolio: This is a real portfolio that for 18 years has followed a simple process of investing in micro-cap value stocks with a management approach requiring a minimum amount of time. It has been used to experiment and provide insight into methods of practical stock portfolio management. For the past 10 years, its compound rate of return, after all costs, was 19.0%. For further explanation of the Shadow Stock Portfolio, see the most recent January, April, July or October issue of the *AAII Journal* or the Model Portfolios area of AAII. com.

Bernstein, Peter L., "Against the Gods: The Remarkable Story of Risk," John Wiley & Sons, 1998. Interesting book about the development of the concepts of risk. Understandable coverage of prospect theory and chaos theory, both of which challenge conventional theories of risk.

Bernstein, Peter L., editor, "The Portable MBA in Investment," John Wiley & Sons, 1995. Very succinct coverage of investment theory with all the formulae. Requires knowledge of statistics, but can be read for the concepts and the math glossed over. Excellent as a reference.

Brinson, Gary, L., Randolph Hood, and

Gilbert Beebower, "Determinants of Portfolio Performance," Financial Analysts Journal, May-June 1991. This is the work that led to emphasis on asset allocation, but has been misunderstood.

Fama, Eugene F., "The Behavior of Stock Market Prices," Journal of Business, January 1965. Early work showing that stock returns are not normally distributed, possibly with infinite variance.

Fama, Eugene F. and Kenneth French, "The Cross-Section of Expected Stock Returns," Journal of Finance, June 1992. This article contains two interesting aspects. First, it supports the growing disillusion with beta as a useful measure. Second, and more importantly, it provides extensive research support for two anomalies in efficient market theory. Small-capitalization stocks provide higher returns than large-capitalization stocks, and the smaller the better. And high value stocks (measured by low price-to-book ratios) provide higher returns than low value stocks, and the greater the value the better.

Kahneman, Daniel and Amos Tversky, "Prospect Theory: An Analysis of Decision Making Under Risk," Economterica, No. 2, 1979. Early work showing that decision-making is often not rational by traditional measures.

Lowenstein, Roger, "When Genius Failed: The Rise and Fall of Long-Term Capital Management," Random House, 2001. The story of the failure of LTCM and the contribution of modern portfolio theory to the collapse.

Malkiel, Burton G., "A Random Walk Down Wall Street," W.W. Norton, 2011. Classic book, updated frequently, covering all aspects of modern portfolio theory, including criticisms. Very enjoyable reading.

Mandelbrot, Benoit, "The Variations of Certain Speculative Prices," Journal of Business, October, 1963. Early work showing stock prices are not normally distributed.

Mayes, Timothy R. and Todd M. Shank, "Financial Analysis With Microsoft Excel," South-Western Cengage Learning, 2010. Explains the background of a wide array of investment concepts and provides examples of how to construct detailed Excel spreadsheets.

McMillan, Lawrence G., "Options as a Strategic Investment, 4th Edition," Prentice Hall Press, 2001. Very complete coverage of option theory and practice.

Shleifer, Andrei, "Inefficient Markets: An Introduction to Behavioral Finance," Oxford University Press, 2000. Discussion of problems with the efficient market hypothesis from an economist's viewpoint.

Stock Superstars Report. A portfolio-oriented stock advisory service published by AAII. See www.stocksuperstars.com for details.

Taleb, Nassim Nicholas, "The Black Swan, 2nd Edition," Random House, 2010. Expansion of the root and impact of fat tails, outliers, and real-world distributions.

95

American Association of Individual Investors (AAII)
www.aaii.com: Financial information, education and resources.

Morningstar.com
www.morningstar.com: Extensive information on mutual funds and ETFs including historical risk and return information.

NAREIT
www.reit.com: Website of the National Association of Real Estate Investment Trusts. Provides list of REITs and statistical information.

Stock Superstars Report
www.stocksuperstars.com: AAII's stock portfolio service.

Wilshire
www.wilshire.com: Source of information and historical data on all the indexes maintained by Wilshire. Source of unweighted indexes and specialty indexes.

Yahoo! Finance
finance.yahoo.com: Resource for a variety of financial information. Extended stock and mutual fund quotes provide price history that can be downloaded into Excel for statistical analysis.